DISCARDED
from the Nashville Public Library

Praise for

Wildcat Memories:
Inside Stories from Kentucky Basketball Greats

"The Wildcats are the greatest common denominator in our state—
the one thing about which one can strike up a conversation almost
anywhere or anytime. And Doug Brunk's *Wildcat Memories* provides
even more great stories to discuss. He covers a wide spectrum of eras
for Big Blue fans both young and old, commemorating a program
whose tradition is passed down from generation to generation."
—Tom Leach, Voice of the Wildcats

"The key to books about Kentucky basketball is picking the right folks
and getting good interviews, and Doug Brunk has done that. *Wildcat
Memories* does a great job of finding people who may not have gotten
the recognition they deserve—people who were behind the scenes, but
still had a hand in developing one of the greatest athletic programs in
all of sports."
—Ryan Clark, author of *Game of My Life: Kentucky Wildcats* and coauthor
of *100 Things Wildcats Fans Should Know & Do before They Die*

"I went to my first Kentucky game in 1966 at Memorial Coliseum,
and instantly became a Big Blue fan. I have been coaching high school
basketball in Virginia for the last thirty years, and have been blessed
to have six of my players wear the blue-and-white uniform of the
Wildcats. These personal stories chronicle all the memories of the great
players who have played at the University of Kentucky through the
years."
—Steve Smith, head basketball coach, Oak Hill Academy

DISCARDED
from the Nashville Public Library

Wildcat Memories

WILDCAT MEMORIES

INSIDE STORIES FROM KENTUCKY BASKETBALL GREATS

DOUG BRUNK

FOREWORD BY DAN ISSEL

UNIVERSITY PRESS OF KENTUCKY

Copyright © 2014 by The University Press of Kentucky

Scholarly publisher for the Commonwealth,
serving Bellarmine University, Berea College, Centre College of Kentucky,
Eastern Kentucky University, The Filson Historical Society, Georgetown
College, Kentucky Historical Society, Kentucky State University, Morehead
State University, Murray State University, Northern Kentucky University,
Transylvania University, University of Kentucky, University of Louisville,
and Western Kentucky University.
All rights reserved.

Editorial and Sales Offices: The University Press of Kentucky
663 South Limestone Street, Lexington, Kentucky 40508-4008
www.kentuckypress.com

Library of Congress Cataloging-in-Publication Data

Brunk, Doug.
  Wildcat memories : inside stories from Kentucky basketball greats / Doug
Brunk ; foreword by Dan Issel.
     pages cm
  Includes bibliographical references and index.
  ISBN 978-0-8131-4700-0 (pbk. : alk. paper) — ISBN 978-0-8131-4702-4 (pdf)
  — ISBN 978-0-8131-4701-7 (epub)
  1. Kentucky Wildcats (Basketball team)—History. 2. University of Kentucky—
Basketball—History. 3. Basketball players—Kentucky—Anecdotes. I. Title.
  GV885.43.U53B78 20144
  796.323'630976947—dc23   2014016213

This book is printed on acid-free paper meeting
the requirements of the American National Standard
for Permanence in Paper for Printed Library Materials.

∞

Manufactured in the United States of America.

Member of the Association of
American University Presses

To my parents,
Bill and Genevieve Brunk,
for their influence and for providing me
with the privilege of living in Kentucky.

Some are born great,
some achieve greatness,
and some have greatness thrust upon 'em.
—Malvolio,
in William Shakespeare's
Twelfth Night

Contents

Foreword   xiii

Introduction   1

I. The 1920s–1950s

1. Basil Hayden   13
2. Wallace ("Wah Wah") Jones   19
3. Charles Martin ("C. M.") Newton   25
4. Cliff Hagan   33
5. Frank Ramsey   41
6. Ed Beck   47
7. Johnny Cox   55

II. The 1960s–1970s

8. Charles ("Cotton") Nash   61
9. Larry Conley   67
10. Dan Issel   73
11. Joe B. Hall   81
12. Mike Pratt   89
13. Kevin Grevey   95
14. Jack ("Goose") Givens   103
15. Rick Robey   109
16. Kyle Macy   115
17. Derrick Hord   123

III. The 1980s–1990s

18. Jim Master   131
19. Roger Harden   137
20. Deron Feldhaus   143
21. Travis Ford   149
22. Jared Prickett   155
23. Jeff Sheppard   161
24. Allen Edwards   169
25. Derek Anderson   175
26. Orlando ("Tubby") Smith   181
27. Marquis Estill   187

IV. The 2000s–2010s

28. Chuck Hayes   195
29. Ravi Moss   201
30. Patrick Patterson   207
31. Darius Miller   213
32. John Wall   217

Acknowledgments   223
Author's Note   227
Notes   229
Index   233

Foreword

I was blessed to have played fifteen years of professional basketball, first with the Kentucky Colonels in the American Basketball Association (ABA) and then with the Denver Nuggets in the National Basketball Association (NBA). But when people see my height and ask if I played basketball, I say, "Yes, at the University of Kentucky!" *That* really gets their attention! Because of its popularity there have been many books written about Kentucky basketball. So when I agreed to a sit-down interview in Los Angeles in 2012 with Doug Brunk for *Wildcat Memories,* I expected it to be just another one of those books. Once Doug emphasized that he was after stories about the people who impacted me during my time playing at UK, that got my interest. I know of no other book that has taken this approach and presented it in a format of firsthand reflections. We are all shaped and influenced by others in some way. So I was happy to participate.

UK fans are going to love this book because it provides a glimpse into the personal lives of some of the program's greatest former players and coaches. Doug got us all to open up. The voices in *Wildcat Memories* are distinctive and unique, just like the people who make up the great UK fan base known as the Big Blue Nation. I was surprised to learn that winning the Kentucky State High School Basketball Tournament meant more to Cliff Hagan than winning the NCAA Tournament or the NBA Championship. And I was moved by the fact that Roger Harden said that Chuck Melcher, the Campus Crusade for Christ director, had the most influence on his personal growth while he was at UK.

I have not lived in Kentucky full time since 1988 and unfortunately only get to visit a few times each year. However, when I walk down the streets in Lexington or Louisville, UK fans greet me like they saw me the day before. In April 2013 I was honored to have my likeness on a Maker's Mark commemorative bottle. During the signing at Keeneland hundreds of people lined up for me to sign their bottles. Bill Thomason, president of Keeneland, remarked, "Only in Kentucky would parents allow their children to skip school to come to a racetrack and get a bottle of bourbon signed!" I was even more amazed that UK fans would be in line for twenty-four hours in the cold and the rain to get the autograph of a player who hadn't worn the blue and white since 1970.

Wildcat Memories is about much more than basketball. It contains reflections on life lessons, character, working through adversity, thoughts about what makes Kentucky unique from a cultural standpoint, and memories about people who helped the former players and coaches interviewed for this book find their way in life. UK basketball is truly unique in how it brings people together. This book celebrates that sense of connection and supports the first few words of Kentucky's state motto, "United We Stand."

Dan Issel
Windsor, Colorado

Introduction

Perhaps the best description of what makes men's basketball at the University of Kentucky so special to citizens of the Bluegrass State came from the late William "Bill" Keightley, a former postal worker from Lawrenceburg, Kentucky, who served forty-eight years as the equipment manager for the storied program.

In a June 2006 interview[1] Keightley, who was affectionately known as "Mr. Wildcat," observed that UK basketball in the Commonwealth "is so big and everybody wants to feel like they're part of something that's successful, and Kentucky basketball has given 'em this, this feeling of satisfaction. About the only other thing we have maybe is the Kentucky Derby."

Wildcat fans, Keightley continued, "are the ones that make us what we are. They make us work harder because you don't want to disappoint 'em. If you lose you have disappointed 'em and you really don't want to do that."

The allegiance of Kentuckians to UK basketball is larger than life, a wide-reaching bond established long before cell phones, Internet connections, and social media. The program's rich history and success—especially during Coach Adolph Rupp's forty-two-year tenure—are well chronicled. But another layer to the relationship between Kentuckians and UK basketball deserves exploration.

In *Wildcat Memories* you will read stories from some of the program's greatest coaches and players, who responded to my invitation to reflect on Kentuckians who provided influence, mentorship, and moral support during their time under the microscope of UK's fan base, known as Big Blue Nation. What follows on these pages are personal essays by select former coaches and players who—in their own words—shine a light on Kentuckians who played an important role in their lives.

You will meet people like the young Lexington couple Armand and Joyce Angelucci, who opened their home to center Dan Issel after he arrived on the campus of UK from Batavia, Illinois, as a homesick freshman. And Larkie Box, a former marine and star athlete from Cynthiana, Kentucky, who mentored Joe B. Hall in sports and good citizenship during his formative years. Box was Hall's junior varsity basketball coach and even taught him how to drive a car. And the late Reverend Albert B. Lee, former head pastor of Greater Liberty Baptist Church in Lexington, who served as a father figure to young forward Jack Givens, a star UK player who lacked an involved father in his own home.

You will learn about how former Kentucky governor Albert Benjamin "Happy" Chandler made phone calls and wrote letters of support to UK center Ed Beck when Beck's wife, Billie, received a diagnosis of inoperable cancer that took her life at the end of his junior year. The two shared a strong Christian faith, and after Billie's death, Governor Chandler invited Beck to the Governor's Mansion in Frankfort, where he showed him the spot where he knelt every day to pray for God's help in leading the Commonwealth.

These are just some of the impactful Kentuckians you will read about in *Wildcat Memories*. In the course of reflecting on their mentors, the sources interviewed for this book share behind-the-scenes stories about UK basketball. For example, forward Cotton Nash details how Coach Rupp conducted practices. Dan Issel describes how he and other teammates would sneak friends into Memorial Coliseum prior to game time—friends who would hide out in phone booths located on the concourse level until the game started. Forward Kevin Grevey recalls a unique lesson he received from Coach Hall aboard an airplane flight about the importance of UK basketball to Kentuckians.

Sources interviewed for this book also share their personal impressions about the Commonwealth of Kentucky. For example, Owensboro, Kentucky, native Cliff Hagan describes a "state pride that resonates from the mountains of Eastern Kentucky to the flat and rolling hills of Western Kentucky. Although the speech is as varied as the bloodlines, the warmth of its people is a common attribute." Georgia native Ed Beck reflects on the "uniqueness of the state in the context of topography, with the mountains and the coal mining regions in the eastern part of the state, which created rugged individualism in many of the communities." Kevin Grevey recalls driving with his family as a boy from his hometown of Hamilton, Ohio, to Lexington. The emerald-green landscape and rolling hills that unfolded before him "felt like a completely different place than what I was used to," he said, a place where people were "proud of their southern heritage." Patrick Patterson, who played high school basketball in West Virginia, characterizes the Kentuckians he met during his three years at UK as "friendly, open, and welcoming to me. They're a giving people, they don't expect anything back in return, and they're always willing to lend a helping hand."

Ever since Coach Rupp's "Fabulous Five" won UK its first NCAA Championship in 1948, UK has been in a position to recruit the best coaches and players to compete for conference and national championships year after year. The bar is set to win. Coaches expect it from their players. Fans expect it from the coaches and the players. With that unforgiving level of expectation comes a certain friction, as well as a tendency for some fans to elevate UK coaches and players to rock star status. Yet while former UK coaches and players featured in this book were celebrated—even worshipped—for their

Adolph Rupp (right) poses with his mentor, former University of Kansas head basketball coach Dr. Forrest ("Phog") Allen. (Courtesy of the University of Kentucky Archives.)

exceptional leadership skills and athleticism, they also drew inspiration from everyday Kentuckians to help them navigate through life.

Wildcat Memories spotlights some of those individuals, people like Seth Hancock, the young owner of Claiborne Farm who hired center Rick Robey to work on the farm during the summers of his UK career. Some people thought Robey had been handed a cushy summer job, but Hancock showed no favoritism. He docked Robey if he showed up late for work and penalized him if he ditched work altogether. "He made me accountable," Robey said of Hancock. "He was one of those pointed types of people who made me a better person not only off the basketball court but on the basketball court as well."

Were it not for the influence of certain Kentuckians, would some of UK's greatest coaches and players have achieved the mark they ultimately made on the basketball program? The question certainly comes up in the case of Dan Issel, who was so homesick his freshman year he nearly packed his bags and returned to his native Illinois. More than once his mentors, the Angeluccis, talked him out of "pulling up stakes" and leaving the program. Issel stayed on and became UK's all-time leading scorer. Such Kentuckians hold a unique place in UK basketball history and deserve recognition for the role they played in the lives of the former coaches and players featured in this book. The magnitude of their influence may be difficult to measure, but these men and women indirectly contributed to the success of the winningest program in college basketball history.

During his sophomore year Kevin Grevey struggled to pull out of a slump, overwhelmed by the pressure of playing basketball at UK. One day he removed himself from the Memorial Coliseum court during a practice, frustrated by his performance. He was missing shots, being outrebounded, and the man he guarded was beating him offensively. Coach Hall entered the locker room to talk with Grevey and asked him to reflect on why he started playing basketball in the first place.

"Because I love basketball," the young Grevey told his coach, whom he considered an important mentor.

"There you go," Coach Hall said. "You've got to have fun and enjoy what you're doing out there on the court, love the game and accept its spoils and rewards. I don't think you're having fun. Take a shower, come back tomorrow, and let's have a better frame of mind. You're putting way too much pressure on yourself."

Grevey viewed that positive reinforcement from Coach Hall as a pivotal moment in his life, and he went on to enjoy an outstanding career in college and in the National Basketball Association. To this day he remains seventh on UK's list of all-time leading scorers.

Coach Rupp often expressed appreciation for two key mentors in his own life: Dr. Forrest C. ("Phog") Allen, his coach at the University of Kansas, and Dr. James Naismith, the man who invented the game of basketball and who coached Dr. Allen during his playing days at the University of Kansas.

In an undated audio interview,[2] Rupp described how Allen strove for perfection and embraced discipline—two traits that would come to define Rupp himself. Dr. Allen "took great pride in his personal appearance," Coach Rupp recalled. "He had to just look the best. And whenever a photograph of the team, a picture, was made, everybody had to just absolutely have a nice haircut, and everything had to be just so. He believed in perfect dress in every respect. He wouldn't put up with any of this sloppy business at all. And that's the kind of a life that he lived." Rupp went on to say that "if we had more men like 'Phog' Allen living today in many places of responsibility, this would be a far better world."

In a May 1971 audio interview,[3] Coach Rupp characterized Dr. Naismith as an approachable, even-keeled teacher. "I'd often go into his office and just sit down and breeze with him," he recalled. "He always had time to talk. He always was interesting. He had a little Canadian accent, and he had a mustache, and always had that twinkle in his eye, you could always tell he was glad to see you, and you could stay just as long as you wanted to, and he had the time for you. I learned a lot from this man. I learned a lot of his philosophy, his philosophy in life, the way he felt about things, and then, of course, he also passed some of this on to Dr. Allen . . . and from the two of them, I got the philosophy of basketball that I now embrace."

Embrace he did. Armed with wisdom from his mentors, Rupp won 82 percent of his games as UK's coach and led the Wildcats to four NCAA National Championships.

I joined the fray of devoted Wildcat fans in the mid-1970s as a boy growing up in Wilmore, Kentucky, fascinated by Kyle Macy's free-throw-shooting form, Rick Robey's rebounding skills, and Jack Givens's scoring prowess. Television broadcasts of games connected me to this unique display of athleticism, teamwork, and gritty competitiveness that UK fans expect season after season. If a game wasn't televised I listened to the legendary play-by-play announcer Cawood Ledford call games on the AM radio, shoddy reception or not. These games and players became topics of conversation with friends at school and at church and with other citizens of the Bluegrass State I met as a youngster, providing us all a ready basis for connection.

My story is far from unique, though. Peel away UK's hallowed halls of Alumni Gym, Memorial Coliseum, and Rupp Arena, the record number of wins, the storied rivalries with the University of Louisville and Indiana University, and the eight NCAA National Championship titles, and what's left is a deep-seated tie to something greater than ourselves. As it turns out, the program's former coaches and players describe a similar sentiment, and they credit certain Kentuckians for helping them along the way. Enjoy their stories.

Part I

The 1920s–1950s

The University of Kentucky men's basketball program was eighteen years old when it won the first Southern Intercollegiate Athletic Association basketball championship with a 20–19 victory over Georgia on March 1, 1921. Staged in Atlanta, the event is considered to be the first college basketball tournament ever played. Following the victory UK's team captain Basil Hayden became the first Wildcat to earn All-American honors in basketball.

Nine years later, a high school coach from Freeport, Illinois, named Adolph Rupp was hired to become head basketball coach of the Wildcats. He led UK to its first national title with a 46–45 win over Rhode Island in the 1946 National Invitational Tournament (NIT) Championship game and to a runner-up finish in the 1947 NIT Championship game. In the following year, a team known as the "Fabulous Five" won UK its first National Collegiate Athletic Association (NCAA) National Championship with a 58–42 victory over Baylor University on March 23, 1948. The Five included Ralph Beard, Wallace ("Wah Wah") Jones, Alex Groza, Kenny Rollins, and Cliff Barker—all of whom earned an Olympic gold medal in London that summer as members of the US basketball team that beat France 65–21 in the finals. Every member of that starting-five team except for Rollins returned for the 1948–1949 season, which culminated in UK repeating as NCAA National Champions with a 46–36 victory against Oklahoma A&M on March 26, 1949. The Wildcats haven't won back-to-back titles since.

UK closed out the 1949–1950 campaign by playing its last game in the 2,800-seat Alumni Gym, which had served as home court since 1924 and where UK had won 247 of 271 games played, setting a foundation to become the winningest college basketball program in the nation. In December 1950, home court moved to the newly constructed Memorial Coliseum, a structure built to seat 11,500 fans, or more than four times the capacity of Alumni Gym. The move proved to be fortuitous; on March 27, 1951, UK won its third NCAA national title, defeating Kansas State 68–58. It also won 129 straight games in Memorial Coliseum until falling to Georgia Tech 59–58 on January 8, 1955.

In 1952 UK was rocked by a point-shaving scandal that resulted in suspension of the basketball program for the entire 1952–1953 season. The NCAA did not permit the Wildcats to compete with other college programs, but they could still practice. In fact, Adolph Rupp held four public intrasquad scrimmages during the suspended season.

During the 1953–1954 campaign the Wildcats ran the table on all opponents, ending the regular season with a 25–0 record overall and a 14–0 record in Southeastern Conference (SEC) play. The season began with Cliff Hagan pouring in fifty-one points against Temple—at that time a school record—and ended with Frank Ramsey scoring thirty points in a 63–56 victory over Louisiana State University to capture that year's SEC championship. Following that win, however, the NCAA ruled that Hagan, Ramsey, and teammate Lou Tsioropoulos were ineligible to participate in the NCAA Tournament because they had already earned their academic degrees from

UK. As a result, Coach Rupp decided that the Wildcats would not compete in that year's tournament.

Four years later a team known as the "Fiddlin' Five" captured another NCAA national title for UK with a 84–72 win over Seattle on March 22, 1958. Senior Vernon Hatton led all scorers with a thirty-point performance. The victory marked the Wildcats' fourth NCAA national title in a span of ten years, which currently stands as an unmatched feat for the program.

1

Basil Hayden

Born in Stanford, Kentucky, Basil Hayden spent his formative years in Paris, Kentucky, where he began playing basketball in the sixth grade and went on to play for Paris High School. At UK, he scored 333 points in thirty-nine games played from 1919 to 1922, for an average of 8.5 points per contest. The forward served as team captain on the Wildcats squad that captured the first-ever Southern Intercollegiate Athletic Association basketball tournament with a 20–19 victory over Georgia on March 1, 1921, an event that is considered to be the first college basketball tournament ever played.

After the tournament Hayden became the first UK basketball player to earn All-American honors. He reflects on that achievement in the following essay, which is based on an audio interview conducted by Hayden's stepdaughter Janie Daugherty on November 30, 1992. Though the subject was not discussed in the audio interview, Hayden was called on to coach UK's basketball team during the 1926–1927 campaign, after the abrupt resignation of Coach Ray Eklund. Hayden's opportunity came just one week before the season formally tipped off. The team's record that year was 3–13. "There wasn't any chance to get any sort of teamwork or anything out of 'em—no time," Hayden told reporter

Basil Hayden (holding the basketball) is pictured with his teammates following UK's first championship in the sport, a 20–19 victory over Georgia in the 1921 Southern Intercollegiate Athletic Association Tournament. The head coach was George C. Buchheit, top left. (Courtesy of the University of Kentucky Archives.)

Brent Kelley in Sports Collectors Digest. [1] *"I got about as famous for coaching the worst losing season as [Adolph] Rupp did for winning."*

   Hayden's lifespan included three centuries. He was born on May 19, 1899, and died on January 9, 2003, at the age of 103.

I grew up with three brothers and two sisters. For the first few years of my life our family lived in a pretty good-sized brick house in Stanford, Kentucky. When we moved to Paris we had a large brick house on the corner of Walker Avenue and Eighth Street. It had French windows in one corner.

   In 1910 we moved into a two-story framed house on Henderson Street. There was no electricity in Paris in 1910, so my father,

Joseph Wallace Hayden, put gas pipes around the house to use gas heat and gas lights. I shared an upstairs bedroom with my father and my mother, Annie Brown Hayden. There were two beds in there. In the winter when it was real cold sometimes I would sleep at the foot of their bed.

My mother had the greatest influence on me growing up. She taught me a lot about honesty and how to treat other people, how to get along with people—general knowledge that a little boy ought to have. She didn't want me to have knives, and she used to be careful about who I played with. She didn't want me playing with boys that were too rough or too ignorant. I was about ten or eleven years old when I got my first knife. I kept it in my pocket most of the time, but Mom knew. You couldn't fool her. She could see where I had carved on things.

I didn't see much of my oldest brother, Leo. He left home around 1910 to live in Louisville. He married a lady there who died in childbirth. Leo was then sent to a hospital unit in France to handle people who were injured during World War I. My mother always thought that the work he did there ruined his heart. In 1930 he was hunting down in Tennessee and dropped dead.

I graduated from Paris High School, and I played basketball there. My mother was anxious for one of her four boys to become a preacher, so she picked me out to be the preacher and sent me to Transylvania College in Lexington. I was interested in studying chemistry, though, so I transferred over to the University of Kentucky as a sophomore and graduated with a degree in industrial chemistry. I also played basketball at UK.

In 1921, UK's basketball team played in the Southern Intercollegiate Athletic Association's first college basketball tournament in Atlanta, Georgia. It was sponsored by the Atlanta Athletic Club and was made up of many of the same teams that are in the present-day Southeastern Conference. We won the tournament in the last game against Georgia by a score of 20–19. Basketball was in its younger days back then, but the newspapers covered the event in great detail. One newspaper reporter who wrote about me did his utmost to make the stories as interesting as possible. I think his stories about me were the thing that made the coaches decide on selecting me as an All-American, being the captain of the team that won that tournament.

After graduating from UK I moved to Detroit, Michigan, to live with my other brother, Ellis, who had graduated from UK with a degree in mechanical engineering and was working in a Dodge automobile factory. I worked at that same Dodge plant in the chemical laboratory analyzing steel, but I got so homesick that I came back to Kentucky in the fall. I went back to school to get enough credits in education so I could teach.

I became a teacher at Clark County High School in Winchester, Kentucky, and coached their basketball and football teams. I also coached basketball at Kentucky Wesleyan College during the 1922–1923 season and then moved on to Stanford High School, where I coached football and baseball.

After that I sold insurance in Richmond, Kentucky. I wasn't very successful as an insurance agent, so I got into the hotel business there. That was at a time when there was a lot of traffic up and down Highway 25^2 going to Florida. When the Great Depression hit that closed off many businesses, including my hotel business. I was out of work for about three years before I got a job at the National Bank and Trust Company in Paris. I worked there for twenty-five years. I started out as a bookkeeper, and I ended up as an executive vice president. I left National Bank and Trust Company in 1957. I was quite relieved to get out of that bank and away from the responsibility of trying to collect money. People don't mind borrowing money, but they're slow about paying it back. It's not a good situation to be in. I was not a tough collector. From there I worked for one year as a state bank examiner, then became treasurer of the Interboard Council, Kentucky Conference of the Methodist Church, and retired from that job in 1976.

Looking back, my mother taught me a lot. Out of what she taught me and what I decided myself, I became a mild-mannered person. A lot of boys liked to fight. I didn't care anything about fighting. I'd run from a fight. I made the best I could of a situation I was in without getting all stirred up about it. I think I accomplished more that way than I accomplished any other way. Of course, one of the outstanding things in my life was basketball, culminating in being chosen an All-American, and the University of Kentucky recognizing me as a person that was outstanding in basketball by retiring my jersey in Rupp Arena and giving me a plaque.

2

Wallace ("Wah Wah") Jones

Harlan, Kentucky, native Wallace ("Wah Wah") Jones is widely considered to be the best all-around athlete in UK history for his standout achievements in basketball, football, and baseball.

Jones, whose nickname came from his younger sister, who struggled to pronounce "Wallace," was a starting forward on the "Fabulous Five" squad, which won UK its first NCAA National Championship in 1948. The starters on that team went on to earn a gold medal as members of the 1948 US Olympic basketball team.

Jones finished his UK basketball career with 1,151 points, which ranks him forty-sixth on the program's list of all-time leading scorers. He is the only UK athlete to have had his jersey retired in both basketball and football.

After graduating from UK, Jones played for the Indianapolis Olympians of the NBA from 1949 to 1952. The following year he was elected sheriff of Fayette County and served one four-year term. In 2012 Jones was inducted into the Kentucky High School Basketball Hall of Fame.

Jones's wife, Edna, predeceased him in 2003. He has three children, Wallace Jr., Vicki, and Ira, and five grandchildren. He is the founder of Blue Grass Tours, and he lives in Lexington.

Wallace ("Wah Wah") Jones (27) earned All-American honors in football playing for Paul ("Bear") Bryant and in basketball playing for Adolph Rupp. (Courtesy of the University of Kentucky Archives.)

I had dreamed about playing basketball at the University of Kentucky for many, many years. When I was growing up in Harlan in the 1940s, our family didn't have a television set. We had a radio, but the reception on that was not reliable. Sometimes we'd get reception in the attic of our house, but often we'd pile in the car and drive into the nearby mountains to listen to UK basketball games on the car radio.

I was lucky to have been part of a winning basketball program at Harlan High School. Our team went to the state tournament four years in a row (1942 to 1945), and in 1944 our team won the state championship title. At the end of my high school career I had scored 2,398 points, which at the time was the highest total by a single high school player in the United States.

Were it not for the man who went on to become my father-in-law—Alva Ball of Middlesboro, Kentucky (I married his daughter, Edna)—I might have ended up playing basketball for the University of Tennessee instead of for UK. In the summer of 1945 Mr. Ball overheard that I was considering signing with Tennessee. I don't know who he called at UK, but the next day a driver arrived in Harlan to transport me to Lexington to meet with Coach Adolph Rupp. After meeting with him I decided to sign at UK, but basketball was not the only sport I played there. I lettered four years in football and three years in baseball.

By the time I arrived in Lexington for my freshman year, the Wildcats had already played one football game. Paul ("Bear") Bryant was the head football coach, and he played me in the second game of the season, even though I didn't know any of the plays or the signals. I played all sixty minutes of that game, on both defense and offense! George Blanda played on that team. Coach Rupp didn't like the fact that I played football. He was worried I would get injured, and he kind of held me back a little bit.

Coach Rupp and Coach Bryant were a lot alike. They both

were tough on their players. During a football game against the University of Cincinnati I got some teeth knocked loose. During a break in the game I said something about this to Coach Bryant. "Well, you don't run on your teeth," he said to me. "Get back in there!" After the game my teammates had a steak dinner at the Cincinnati Netherland Plaza hotel, and I was sucking on a milkshake.

Coach Rupp and Coach Bryant expected the best out of you. You couldn't slack off, that's for sure. I had no trouble with either one of them; they were no-nonsense people. After one of my baseball seasons at UK I was invited to try out with the Boston Braves, which is the Major League Baseball team now known as the Atlanta Braves. I told this to Coach Bryant, and he asked me point blank, "Are you going to play football, or are you going to play baseball?"

"I guess I'll play football, Coach," I replied. I was scared to say anything.

During my sophomore year in basketball I was matched up in a game against my brother, Hugh, who was a star player at the University of Tennessee. UK won, of course. At that game my mother said she felt like the president of the United States at the army-navy football game; she was ready to move from one side to the other.

I was voted most popular freshman during my first year at UK. A lot of people had followed me from my high school career and rooted for me. I enjoyed their favoritism, but it surprised me to be that popular. That popularity helped me in my later business career and in my bid for election as sheriff of Fayette County, which I won in 1953. I was the first Republican sheriff in Fayette County since the Civil War, and there hasn't been one since.

Many people helped me during my career at UK, including residents of Harlan. Everybody was so good to me. There were a number of people who would come to our games to cheer me on. Others would send letters of support. I also got to know a lot of peo-

ple in the Thoroughbred industry. In fact, I had a summer job working the horse sales at Keeneland.

I think the UK fan base is so strong because of the program's
long-standing winning tradition. During my UK career we played
all of our home games in Alumni Gym, which could only seat about
twenty-eight hundred people. During my four years we won 130
out of 140 games. That kept the winning tradition at UK going. I
enjoyed it.

3

Charles Martin ("C. M.") Newton

*After serving as a reserve guard/forward for the Wildcats basket-
ball team from 1949 to 1951 and as a pitcher for the baseball team,
C. M. Newton launched a basketball coaching career that spanned three
decades at three different institutions. He began in 1956 at Transylvania College (where he recruited that program's first African American
player), followed by coaching stints at the University of Alabama (where
he recruited that program's first African American player and led the
Crimson Tide to three straight SEC titles) and at Vanderbilt University, before returning to his alma mater in 1989 to become UK's athletic
director, a post he held for eleven years.*

*Newton is widely credited with navigating the resurrection of
UK's basketball program after the NCAA imposed three years' proba-
tion and other sanctions following the 1988–1989 season. He also hired
Bernadette Mattox as UK's first African American women's basketball
coach (in 1995) and Orlando ("Tubby") Smith as the university's first
African American men's basketball coach (in 1997).*

Newton served as president of USA Basketball from 1992 to

After his UK playing career Charles ("C. M.") Newton coached at Transylvania College, Alabama, and Vanderbilt, earning a win-loss record of 500–374. (Courtesy of the University of Kentucky Archives.)

1996, and he helped select the US Olympic "Dream Team" of 1992. In 2000 he was inducted into the Naismith Memorial Basketball Hall of Fame. He currently lives in Tuscaloosa, Alabama, and is a member of the National Invitational Tournament Selection Committee. The football field at UK's Commonwealth Stadium bears his name.

Having grown up in Fort Lauderdale, Florida, I had never seen snow before I went to Kentucky. Being in such a different environment was quite a culture shock to me. In fact, there were times I was so homesick that I thought of leaving the program and returning to Florida. My teammate Ralph Beard and our team manager, Humsey Yessin, talked me out of that. They'd say things like, "You don't want to leave Kentucky" and "We're here for you." So I stayed.

As a player I never had a significant impact because I was a substitute. But I always felt a part of something really big. The fact that I played on the 1951 national championship team, the fact that I made the travel squad, and that I was one of the first substitutes off the bench, made it palatable for me.

Coach Rupp was very important to me because he motivated in a different way than what I was accustomed to. He motivated by fear, mostly, but he was an outstanding basketball coach. I never did break through that fear of Coach Rupp. For example, I'm the only player that ever played for Coach Rupp who went on to coach against him and won. This was in 1972, during my third year as coach of the men's basketball team at the University of Alabama. We beat the Wildcats 73–70 on our home court. Coach Rupp always considered former players as "one of his boys." You never were a peer, but I wanted to be a coaching peer of his. When our Alabama team beat him that day, I thought that might be a breakthrough on the way to that goal, but it wasn't. After our win he congratulated me and said we deserved to win. Then he said, "But . . ."—and with that

I was transported right back to the player-coach relationship. "You're trying to do too much offensively," he told me. "You need to simplify your offense." He wasn't being critical; that was just his nature.

My freshman year as a player for UK was Coach Harry Lancaster's first as a full-time assistant coach. Coach Lancaster actually did more teaching than Coach Rupp did. He was very good to me over the years, and very demanding. He became UK's baseball coach my junior year, and I was a member of that team. He was a taskmaster, but he was great to be around. I enjoyed him a great deal.

My teammates and I were student-athletes in the truest sense of the word. We were expected to come in and perform well in basketball as athletes, and we were expected to earn a degree in four years. Today's players are much more coddled and recruited and different in that respect. I never will forget our transition from the 2,800-seat Alumni Gym, where I played until my junior year, to the 11,500-seat Memorial Coliseum. At the time many people thought Memorial Coliseum was just too big. "They'll never fill it up," critics said. But they did. There were similar sentiments expressed by critics and even by some coaches when Rupp Arena was built. Yet today, it's difficult to find an open seat at any UK game played there.

I was the head men's basketball coach at Vanderbilt University in 1989 when I got a phone call from UK's then-president Dr. David P. Roselle asking if I would consider becoming UK's athletic director in the wake of an NCAA probation. I had no thought of leaving Vanderbilt for UK or anyplace else. But Dr. Roselle convinced me not only that I was wanted as the athletic director but that I was needed. It was the "needed" part that really got to me because UK had been so good to me over the years. They'd provided me an opportunity to receive an education and to play basketball. I had become a successful basketball coach because of my experience there. So off I went to UK.

I knew that the most important decision I would make as ath-

"They'll never fill it up," naysayers said prior to the opening of Memorial Coliseum as the new home court for UK basketball. (Courtesy of the University of Kentucky Archives.)

letic director at UK was the naming of a basketball coach, because if we got the wrong person we'd go the way of UCLA in the post–John Wooden era. Yet if we got the right person we would not miss a beat. Rick Pitino was exactly the right person for the job because I wanted an outsider, and I wanted someone who had experienced the tough aspect of media scrutiny. What better person could you have than the former coach of the New York Knicks? When it became obvious to me that Rick was really interested in leaving the Knicks for

UK, I felt like he could come in and handle the media and the fan base, which he did. Rick is the best coach I've ever been around—bar none—in any sport. He's the whole package. He came into that program and, from day one, gave us not only an honest program—a straightforward program with rules—but a championship type of a program, because that's the only way he knows to do it. I'll always be grateful to him. He made me a good AD.

I got some criticism for hiring Rick initially because one of his early rules with players was that they could have no adult friends except the coaching staff. I had some high-powered boosters and others who came barreling into my office wondering what was going on. I also remember some fans being wary of Rick because of his heavy New York accent. I urged people not to judge Rick by how he talked and reminded them that Coach Rupp talked differently, too —with a midwestern nasal twang—and he'd had pretty good suc-cess as a coach. Rick, Dr. Roselle, and his successor, Dr. Charles T. Wethington, were very meaningful to me during my time as athletic director at UK. Tubby Smith was also very important because in 1997 I hired him to become the first African American men's head coach at UK. He did a great job.

The Big Blue Nation is fanatical about UK basketball. The way I see it, their level of devotion is on par with that of fans who follow Alabama Crimson Tide football. They are great fans in every respect of the word. Sometimes I felt like they took it too seriously and took it over the line, and yet you'd rather have that than have them be indifferent. People really care about Kentucky basketball. The Big Blue Nation includes people from all walks of life: alumni, bankers, coal miners, and even some who have never set foot on campus in Lexington. It doesn't matter; they're Kentucky fans.

I am also proud of the accomplishments relative to football during my tenure as AD. With Jerry Claiborne's retirement, we were able to hire Bill Curry from the University of Alabama program, and

Bill did a very good job in the early years, leading us to the Peach Bowl in Atlanta versus Clemson. He was replaced by Hal Mumme, who brought in the Air Raid offense from Valdosta State. Hal led us to the Outback Bowl versus Penn State, then the Music City Bowl versus Syracuse. During this time we were able to renovate Commonwealth Stadium and add seats and boxes and a new playing field. It became a great stadium for football, and we were able to sell it out. During my tenure UK also built new soccer and softball stadiums, built a new outdoor tennis center, renovated the baseball field, built new coaching offices for football at Nutter Training Center, and built the Nutter Field House. We left the university in a debt-free financial position since all the improvements were paid for except the stadium expansion, which was paid for in gate receipts. I am very proud of these accomplishments and would like to express thanks to my former administrative staff: Larry Ivy, Gene DeFilippo, Kathy Deboor, Bob Bradley, John Cropp, Russ Pear, Mickey King, Kyle Moats, and all the coaches involved.

4

Cliff Hagan

Owensboro, Kentucky, native Cliff Hagan led the Owensboro High School Red Devils to the Kentucky State High School Basketball Championship in 1949, scoring 41 points in the title game. At UK the center scored 1,475 points in seventy-seven games that he played between 1950 and 1954, ranking him as the program's seventeenth all-time leading scorer (an average of 19.2 points per game). He also ranks third on the list of the program's career leaders in rebounds (1,035, or an average of 13.4 per game).

Famous for his hook shot, Hagan was a member of UK's 1951 NCAA National Championship team, which defeated Kansas State 68–58. A two-time consensus All-American, he led the 1953–1954 Wildcats with an average of twenty-five points per game in UK's only undefeated season (25–0).

After his UK career Hagan was drafted by the Boston Celtics but served two years in the US Air Force as a first lieutenant. Before his discharge the Celtics traded him to the St. Louis Hawks along with Ed Macauley for the draft rights to Bill Russell. Hagan spend his entire ten-year NBA career in St. Louis and was a member of the 1958 NBA Championship squad. He finished his career averaging eighteen points per game.

A two-time consensus All-American, Cliff Hagan led the 1953–1954 Wildcats in scoring, with an average of twenty-five points per game. That season the Wildcats finished with a 25–0 record. (Courtesy of the University of Kentucky Archives.)

Hagan served as UK's athletic director from 1975 to 1988, and in 1978 he became the first Wildcat to be inducted into the Naismith Memorial Basketball Hall of Fame. In 1993 the UK baseball stadium was named in his honor. The Boys and Girls Club in Owensboro also bears his name. Today he and his wife, Martha, maintain homes in Lexington and in Vero Beach, Florida.

There is something special about Kentucky and Kentuckians—a state pride that resonates from the mountains of Eastern Kentucky to the flat and rolling hills of Western Kentucky. Although the speech is as varied as the bloodlines, the warmth of its people is a common attribute, not just among "true blue" UK fans but among all who dream of victories for "our team."

There are probably more misconceptions about our state than any other. Do not underestimate our folk because of accent. Intelligence or lack of it is innate and not book-learned. Perfect English does not guarantee good decisions. The Bluegrass State is not too big or too small, but just right and perfect for rearing a family. The sun continues to shine bright for me "on my old Kentucky home"!

In the 1940s the University of Kentucky men's basketball program was on a pedestal all by itself: back-to-back NCAA Championships plus a National Invitational Championship in New York. Kentucky was the mecca of collegiate basketball. This is not to say that other in-state schools were not representative. The University of Louisville, Eastern Kentucky University, Western Kentucky University, Morehead State University, and Murray State University had good basketball coaches and programs. This was before television and, in particular, cable TV and ESPN, so fandom occurred via radio. The Wildcats had the Ashland Oil Radio Network, which covered the entire state and fed the hungry fanatics. Alumni Gym only seated less than three thousand, yet UK won two NCAA Championships with that facility as home court.

My family did not listen to University of Kentucky games or attend any of my high school games. I visited the University of Louisville, Western Kentucky University, Indiana University, and the University of Notre Dame with alumni. This was before the "official visit," where today's stars are lavishly entertained and scrutinized. Most everyone knew I was bound for Lexington. My high school team, the Owensboro Red Devils, won the 1949 Kentucky State High School Basketball Championship by beating Lexington's Lafayette Generals, where I broke the long-standing scoring record with forty-one points. The previous record was twenty-nine and held for twenty more years. Nothing, including NCAA and NBA championships, has ever meant as much to me as that state trophy. Somehow, the first breakthroughs are the most precious! As a result of my play in that state tourney, I was invited along with a later Kentucky teammate, Frank Ramsey of Madisonville, to fly to New York City the next day to watch the Wildcats win the Eastern Finals of the NCAA tourney in the old wonderful Madison Square Garden. After watching the "Fabulous Five" in action, starry-eyed, I was a captured Wildcat.

I come from a large family—six boys and four girls—that was reduced by enlistments for service during World War II. As a result I became the eldest and therefore the leader of my remaining four siblings at the tender age of ten. Having a place to spend time is essential for any youngster, and the local YMCA was my refuge, just a ten-block walk away. Of course, the basketball court was my lure and escape. As I added inches to my stature and prowess to my skills, my local reputation was enhanced. Grade school and then junior high basketball became paramount in my life. Perfect attendance certificates also loomed large. That is why I am so proud of the Cliff Hagan Boys and Girls Club in

Owensboro, which provides a special haven for inner-city kids and others.

The first person outside of my immediate family that influenced my life was my junior high homeroom teacher, Miss Mary Nancy Wilson. She arranged my first and needed dental appointment and later provided counseling and guidance eagerly sought by any youngster. In high school she began saving newspaper clippings, which eventually culminated in four large albums that she presented to me and my future wife as we finished college. What a time-consuming task and commitment that still warms my heart, since I married my high school sweetheart, Martha Jean Milton, on September 4, 1954.

The manager of the local radio station, WOMI, Hugh Potter Sr., and his wife, Cliffordean, and their son, Hugh, my lifelong pal and friend, recognized my potential, nurtured my self-esteem, and enlarged my vistas. Others, including a local sports broadcaster, Army Armstrong, a home builder, Bill Thompson, and an attorney and UK alumnus, Bill Gant, took special interest in my budding career.

No one was more instrumental and important to me than my high school basketball coach, "Big Mac" Laurence McGinnis, a former Wildcat at UK who predated "the Baron," Adolph Rupp. With his quiet leadership and presence Coach McGinnis guided our 1949 Owensboro Red Devils to the Kentucky High School State Championship. Is anything bigger than that to a young boy growing up in Kentucky?

The Big Blue Nation (BBN) is a relatively new term picked up by the media regarding our unique fandom. The support has grown as the media support has increased dramatically. First it was local radio, then statewide networks and beyond. Local television, statewide networks, and then national coverage, with cable reigning supreme. Then ESPN came along, and it all exploded exponentially.

Fans were able to follow every game, every coach's utterance, every rising star's perspiration so closely that they were hooked vicariously for life.

Basketball tournament selection committees know that the BBN will show up in droves to buy tickets and expand the economy of the host city's venue. Future recruits are not unaware of this strong relationship. We always knew we could count on the cheerleaders, pep band, and BBN to provide an edge at every arena. That is why the home court is worth ten points! I always felt we were bigger, stronger, and more dominant because of our diehard fans. For many years, our on-campus Memorial Coliseum was one of the largest arenas in the country. Now Rupp Arena, although aging, still rivals most other home courts.

In the 1952–1953 basketball season our basketball team was given what was later to become known as the "Death Penalty" by the NCAA Infractions Committee, which disallowed us from playing any games in our conference that year. Coach Rupp countered by suggesting that we might just play a schedule wholly outside the SEC. The finding was changed to prevent us from playing any other teams. As a result, we practiced hard and long all season long, which was no fun at all, because the only fun ever in practice was when we scrimmaged. Otherwise, practice was a drag! Coach Rupp was apparently aware of this and came up with the novel idea of four public scrimmages on our home court in Memorial Coliseum by dividing the teams into the Hagans versus the Ramseys, Blue versus White, and so forth. No one could have possibly anticipated the excitement and expectation that surrounded these three public displays of Kentucky's future talent, destined to become the University of Kentucky's only undefeated team. The fans must have sensed something, because to our utter amazement, the hungry fans filled Memorial Coliseum to the roof for all four scrimmages, therefore drawing the largest crowds to see a basketball game that year in the entire South. Our team went 25–0 and assuaged the hungry appetite of the most ardent Wildcat fans!

To this day I continue to think that I was placed in some kind of a role-model status as a varsity athlete, and this assumption only grew as I progressed in my game. The idea that athletes are not role models is ludicrous. I always felt that I was representing not only my family and school but also my city and my state and those fans everywhere that cared. Careful not to get carried away, I was constantly aware that it was still just a game. I knew back home that my junior high teacher-mentor was watching and listening. My mom and little brother and sisters were looking up to me. The fans back home continued to be vigilant. New fans here and there came aboard. But somehow, in some places in Kentucky and in other parts of our country, this game is often elevated beyond James Naismith's wildest expectations for an activity that was birthed in a small YMCA in Springfield, Massachusetts, by this Canadian in 1891—an activity that filled the void between football and baseball seasons. In 2014 the NCAA men's Final Four was staged in Cowboys Stadium in Arlington, Texas, which has a seating capacity of eighty thousand. Maybe this round ball is more than just a game after all.

5

Frank Ramsey

Raised in Madisonville, Kentucky, guard Frank Ramsey was a member of UK's 1951 NCAA Championship squad, which defeated Kansas State 68–58. A small forward/guard who earned All-American honors three times, Ramsey scored 1,344 points during his three-year career, ranking him twenty-seventh on the list of the program's all-time leading scorers. Ramsey also pulled down an average of 11.4 rebounds per game, ranking him UK's second all-time in that category, behind Dan Issel. Affectionately known the "Kentucky Colonel," he also played baseball at UK.

In 1953 the Boston Celtics selected Ramsey in the first round of the NBA draft, and he went on to win seven NBA Championships in his nine seasons with that franchise. He finished his NBA career averaging 13.4 points per game, and in 1970 he served one year as head coach of the ABA's Kentucky Colonels.

In 1982 Ramsey became the second Wildcat to be inducted into the Naismith Memorial Basketball Hall of Fame. Today he is president of Dixon Bank in Dixon, Kentucky. He and his wife, Jean, have three children, six grandchildren, and two great-grandchildren. The couple lives in Madisonville.

After his UK career, Frank Ramsey became famous as a "sixth man" star for Boston Celtics coach Red Auerbach. (Courtesy of the University of Kentucky Archives.)

I was born in the little town of Corydon, Kentucky, which had a population of about three hundred. Joseph Chandler—the father of Albert Benjamin ("Happy") Chandler, who went on to become Kentucky's governor—lived two doors up from us. He was the postmaster, and most every day he would push me in a wheelbarrow on his way to the train station to pick up the mail. Once we reached the train station he'd put the mail in the wheelbarrow, and I'd walk back home with him. When I was five years old we moved to Madisonville, and I've lived there ever since.

Kentucky is unique because it's a collection of many small towns. Consequently you get to know practically everybody in town. When I was growing up the population of Madisonville was probably five thousand. At that time, if you misbehaved at school you had to watch out when you got home because the teachers knew you and they knew your family. If you got in trouble at school the teacher would call your family. Because of this we didn't have any major behavior-related problems in the schools then. The discipline was there.

My parents, Sara and Frank Ramsey Sr., were the main ones who guided me early in life. They were strict disciplinarians. I certainly didn't want to do anything that upset them. Most of the people I grew up with had to work, not only because their families needed the money but also because there were not enough adult men around to do the work. Most of them were off serving as soldiers in World War II. Also, there wasn't anything else to do. We didn't have television. My father owned a farm and ran a dry goods store. He would put me to work on the farm every summer because he didn't have enough farmhands. I was driving a team of mules and doing a full man's work when I was about ten years old. I also dug ditches for Madisonville, and I painted. It was a completely different atmosphere from nowadays.

When you grow up in a small town like I did, there are other people besides your parents that you come to admire. I think of my high school basketball coach, Gene Tate, who was also a chemistry teacher; my football coach, Ray Ellis, who went on to be an assistant coach at Georgia Tech; and my baseball coach, Orel Caywood, who was also the shop teacher. I was with them so much that they had an influence on my life. They were teachers, and they were role models. They expected you to do your lessons. You didn't want to disappoint them.

During my junior and senior years at Madisonville High School the UK basketball team had won the NCAA Championship twice. There was no television at the time, so we all listened to the games on the radio. Lexington was a four-hour drive from Madisonville. I'd go up there to visit friends of mine I grew up with who were playing football at UK. When Coach Adolph Rupp offered me a scholarship to play basketball there, I jumped at it. At that time pro ball wasn't even in the future thinking of basketball players like me. We went to college to get an education, in addition to playing the sport. At the same time, since UK was a land-grant college every student had to serve two years in the Reserve Officer Training Corps (ROTC). I served with the Army Military Police Corps at an army prison and at Fort Knox.

There were only about five thousand students at UK when I attended, so I didn't have the sense that I was playing for the entire state. At that time UK was the biggest university in Kentucky, and it had the greatest coach in Adolph Rupp. I was playing for the school and for the team. As basketball players we didn't get any special treatment. We didn't have luxurious living quarters like the players do now. We lived in the dorm like everybody else and ate in the dining hall like everybody else. We were normal students. One semester our basketball team had better than a B average. A lot of the people I attended classes with went on to become governors, bankers, doctors, lawyers, and politicians, and I'm still friends with them.

Coach Rupp and Assistant Coach Harry Lancaster ran our practices, and the team managers refereed the scrimmages. When practice started at 3:15 p.m., if you weren't in Memorial Coliseum, the gate was locked. Picture 11,500 empty seats and the players not talking. All you could hear was the bounce of the basketball and the instruction from the coaches. Coach Rupp was at one end of the court, and Coach Lancaster was at the other end. Any time you made a mistake you knew it because they'd tell you. Some of what they said was funny. One of the players, C. M. Newton, was one year ahead of me. He made a mistake in practice one day. Coach Rupp stopped practice and instructed C. M. to sit at his feet. He said to him: "Newton, you're a Shetland pony in a stud horse derby!" During another practice we were going through defensive drills all day. My All-American teammate Cliff Hagan—who was also my college roommate—did something wrong, and the coaches chewed him out something awful. We were all bent over trying to catch our breath, and Coach Rupp told Cliff, "Well, you don't make All-American on defense."

Coach Rupp and Coach Lancaster were hard-drivers, but they were fair. As a coach you've got to be a hard-driver. Kids expect a certain amount of discipline. If you don't have discipline on a team, whether it's basketball, football, baseball, or soccer, you're not going to win. One thing Coach Rupp had was respect from his players. I don't think it was fear, but we all wanted to please him, and we wanted to win.

It may seem hard to believe today, but some UK students stopped coming to our basketball games because we won so much. One of my greatest fears as a player was that we would lose the first home game in Memorial Coliseum. We did not lose a single home game when I was playing there. I constantly keep in touch with my former teammates. It's like we've never been parted. I see Cliff [Hagan] all the time. Another one of our teammates, Bobby Watson, lives in Owensboro. I see him. I also keep in contact with Billy Evans, Gayle Rose, and Lou Tsioropoulos. We're friends as well as teammates. Coach Rupp and I were friends well after my playing days. I'd go in to Lexington and see him up until he died. It was the same way with Harry Lancaster.

I may have earned a bachelor's degree in business from UK, but I earned a doctorate athletically. I played baseball, and I played basketball for one of the greatest coaches ever. Coach Rupp dealt in fundamentals. He taught you how to play the game of basketball. That afforded me a living in the NBA after I completed my military service, and I later used the business education I received at UK to open a bank. I'm grateful for that.

6

Ed Beck

Former UK center Ed Beck nearly signed with Duke University before committing to the Wildcats in 1954. He captained the 1956–1957 squad and the 1957–1958 squad—a team known as the "Fiddlin' Five," which won UK's fourth NCAA National Championship. That same year he was named the Southeastern Conference's Defensive Player of the Year. Beck pulled down 380 rebounds during the 1956–1957 campaign, ranking him as the eighth single-season leader in rebounds in UK history. His average that year was 14.1 rebounds per game.

Following his UK career Beck turned down offers to play professional basketball, opting instead to join an evangelical mission to Asia with Venture for Victory, a team of Christian basketball players. After the tour he enrolled at Asbury Theological Seminary in Wilmore, Kentucky, and completed his ministerial training at the Candler School of Theology in his native Georgia.

Beck spent his entire working career in Christian ministry, including pastorates in Nashville, Denver, Colorado Springs, and Sun City West, Arizona.

Now retired, Beck and his wife, Faye, live in Sun City West. They

Ed Beck (left) holds the NCAA Championship trophy after UK defeated Seattle University 84–72 on March 22, 1958, while teammate Vernon Hatton and Coach Adolph Rupp look on. (Courtesy of the University of Kentucky.)

have four sons, Jonathan Edward, Stephen, Bradley, and Daniel, and seven grandchildren.

When I think of Kentucky I think of my wife, Faye, who was born in Newport, Kentucky, so her roots are there. We've been married since August 27, 1960, so that's one of the thoughts I certainly have of the state. I also think of the uniqueness of the state in the context of its topography, with the mountains and the coal mining regions in the eastern part of the state, which created rugged individualism in many of the communities. Some of my UK teammates came from the mountain regions.

I lived in Kentucky before the interstate highways were built. The travel was challenging at best. These areas of the state lent themselves to isolationism. It was interesting how the coal mining industry shaped people. Then you move to the central part of the state, the Lexington area and the fantastic beauty of the farms, which I was shaped by when I was recruited to play basketball at Kentucky. In fact, when I got off of the plane during my first visit to Lexington as a recruit, the basketball staff didn't take me to the university first; they took me to a horse farm to show me the uniqueness of that country, the beauty of the land. The horse farms at that time were picturesque in every way; the white picket fences and the barns where the horses were kept were better than any house I'd ever lived in.

When I was being recruited by different universities, making trips to different campuses, the hosts were all very cordial and positive in many ways. But UK was different. After Adolph Rupp officially invited me to play basketball at the university, I started getting letters from all over the country, even some from the Philippines and places in Asia—all from people who had graduated from UK. The letters contained words to the effect of *I understand you are considering going to the University of Kentucky. I hope you will make that deci-*

sion. I want you to know that every time you put on the uniform and play for the university—though I will not be in attendance, because I no longer live in the area—I will be pulling for you, and you will be a part of my thoughts. I was a seventeen-year-old kid from Fort Valley, Georgia, and that was a tremendous mind trip.

I found out later that such letter-writing campaigns were the brainchild of Helen King, who was the head of the UK Alumni Association at the time. Any time an athlete was recruited and the school didn't think it was going to land that athlete, the alumni association put the full-court press on. I did not know Helen until I arrived at the university. She had a gregarious, bubbly personality and was totally focused and committed to the university. She had built a social network long before social media. That was impactful. I thought, "If people are that committed to their university, it's more than just an academic institution—as good as it is academically." There was vibrancy at UK that I did not encounter as I visited other schools as a recruit.

After signing with UK I became very close to my teammates because of the crisis situation with Billie, my first wife, a nurse who died from cancer at the end of our 1956–1957 season in Macon, Georgia, where she had been receiving cancer treatment. She was only twenty-four years old, and I was twenty-one. The ordeal had been difficult for me, and my teammates became very involved in my situation in the sense of total support. I'll never be able to say enough about Adolph Rupp and Assistant Coach Harry Lancaster in the sense of their unbelievable support, either. Coach Rupp had met with Billie personally on campus before the 1956 season began, so he knew her and cared for her deeply. He had been impressed by her professionalism as a nurse and how she knew exactly what was happening to her as her cancer progressed. He was a very sensitive person, which did not come across in his public persona. From that time on my whole relationship with Coach Rupp changed, not in the context of the athletic world—I was treated the same as any other athlete on the team—but I became captain of the team my junior and senior years. Coach was very close to his captains, and he communicated to his teams through that person. If anybody had a beef on the team, it was the captain's responsibility to bring those issues before the team and before the coach.

After Billie died, Coach Rupp and Coach Lancaster drove from Lexington to Fort Valley to attend her memorial service. Naturally, I was deeply appreciative of their efforts and all that symbolized to her and to me. I did not expect that, and yet, in reflection afterward, I wasn't surprised. They wanted to me to understand their affection not only for Billie but for me as well. They expressed their condolences and then told me that the next night in Lexington would be the annual basketball banquet. I told them I would not be able to make it, and they understood that. They said they would be thinking about me, and that was all that was said.

When I got back to Lexington my teammates gathered around me and shared what had happened at the banquet. It had been a time of celebration. We had not won the national championship that year, but we had gotten close. It was reported to me that Adolph got up during the banquet and talked about Billie and what she had meant to the team, and what the memory of her was going to mean for the next year. He dedicated the 1957–1958 team to her memory and to her legacy. That team won the NCAA National Championship.

Two other prominent Kentuckians reached out to show me support during Billie's illness and after she died: Albert Benjamin ("Happy") Chandler,[1] who was Kentucky's governor at the time and the biggest supporter of Kentucky basketball I knew, and Frank Graves Dickey,[2] who was the president of UK. I met Happy after a basketball game my freshman year. At that time the freshmen could not play on the varsity team; they had their own schedule. Not many people would come to freshman games, but Happy was one of them. He was an ardent fan and a close friend of Adolph Rupp's.

Happy's style was to watch the game in the stands, and then he would come back to the dressing room afterward to thank us and hug us. He was a hugger. He had this very contagious personality—that's why they called him Happy—but he would hug you and say, "God love you." He always had words of admiration to say, whether we won or lost. During my junior year I was voted Most Valuable Player of the Sugar Bowl Tournament in New Orleans, which our team won. As I reached the edge of the court on my way to the dressing room, Happy Chandler greeted me, and he was elated. He hugged me and showered "God love you" and many of his other common sayings on me. We walked together into the dressing room, and he just kept on talking about the performance of the whole team.

Happy learned about Billie's illness from Coach Rupp. He called me during the basketball season to share his concern and his support, though I don't remember the exact content of the conversation. After Billie's death he invited me over to the Governor's Mansion in Frankfort for a late breakfast. That's when he shared with me how he walked into his office every morning and got down on his knees to ask God's help for the day, and he showed me the very spot where he knelt down. That was a heady situation for a nineteen-year-old who wanted to go into the ministry. He also shared with me the story about the death of his mother, and how that had impacted his life and how her memory was very strong within him, and how he knew that would be true for my situation with Billie.

Frank Dickey also influenced me. He was a gentleman's gentleman and off the charts when it came to not just his leadership capabilities and qualities as the president of the university, but his style. Mr. Dickey would call me to request that I come by and see him in his office, which I did, to just sit with me and share his concern about Billie's situation as a friend, not as the president of the University of Kentucky. He and Happy Chandler impacted my life as very visible public people in leadership capacities in the state of Kentucky who went out of their way to embrace me and support and sustain me. I corresponded with Mr. Dickey until a couple of years before he died.

As basketball instructors, Coaches Rupp and Lancaster were a unique duo. Coach Rupp may have been the architect of the team, but Coach Lancaster was the one who would be on the court teaching the players. Coach Rupp was the PR guy, the emotional guy. For example, when time out was called during a game, we'd go to the sidelines, and Coach Lancaster would say, "This is what's happening," while Coach Rupp would say, "Let's go out and get 'em!" That was their tandem style. If somebody was going to be chewed out, Coach Lancaster chewed them out. Then Coach Rupp would soothe them over. If Coach Rupp would explode at halftime and ream somebody, at the end of the game Coach Lancaster would come in, put his arm around that player, and say, "Hey. You're doing all right." That was their style. They spent an awful lot of time studying the psychological makeup of their players—not just the athletic makeup but how you push a player's buttons and so forth. Back then players stayed at the university for four years. There was no going to the pros early. If you left, you left of your own accord.

Coach Rupp loved jokes. He had a four-tiered cabinet in his office filled with all kinds of jokes and stories that he'd torn out of magazines or people had sent him over the years. He always wanted to compile them and put them in a book of humor. It was an interesting side hobby of his. But when you heard him speak it was one story after the other, usually in the context of athletic folklore or experiences he'd had with Phog Allen and people of his past.

Even after I graduated from the UK I would go by to see Coach Rupp and his wife. We would just sit and talk. His home was always open to me when I was traveling through Lexington. When Faye gave birth to our first son, Jonathan Edward, Coach Rupp mailed us a letter of congratulations within days. "You don't realize how much fun you will have with him and I know he will grow up into a fine fellow," Coach Rupp wrote. "We've got a scholarship waiting for him so see that he gets to be about 6'8" by the time he is 18."

In the fall of 2008 Faye and I traveled to Lexington to attend the fiftieth anniversary of our 1958 national championship team. We had a meal together and were celebrated during halftime of a home game in Rupp Arena. At the end of the game, as fans were milling around to talk to us, I had probably a dozen people come up to me over the course of an hour and say, "Ed, I saw you play every game at Memorial Coliseum."

"Every game?" I replied. "That was over fifty years ago!"

"I saw you play all four years," they said.

This sentiment was shared by men and women in their seventies. Some were in their eighties. To me that was unreal.

Earlier that day, well before tip-off, Faye and I walked around downtown Lexington, as we hadn't been there for years. On three separate occasions people came out of the stores and said, "You're Ed Beck."

"Yes, I am," I replied.

They'd say things like, "Thank you for all you did for the university."

I don't know about the legacy at places like UCLA or Notre Dame, but the unbelievable commitment by Kentuckians to UK and to all of its athletic programs, especially basketball, is overwhelming. I don't know quite how to explain that type of bleeding blue, but that was a phrase I grew up with at the university, and it's true. It's very, very true.

7

Johnny Cox

During his senior year at Hazard High School, Neon, Kentucky, native Johnny Cox scored thirty-two points in the Bulldogs' 74–66 win over the Adair County Indians in the 1955 Kentucky High School Athletic Association boys' state basketball championship game. Following that contest Cox was named the state's "Mr. Basketball."

During his three-year career at UK, Cox scored 1,461 points, which ranks him nineteenth all-time in scoring. He scored 24 points and grabbed sixteen rebounds in UK's 84–72 win over Seattle on March 22, 1958, to secure the program's fourth NCAA National Championship. He led UK in scoring during the 1956–1957 and 1958–1959 campaigns, averaging 19.4 and 17.9 points per game, respectively.

An exceptional rebounder, Cox pulled down 1,004 rebounds as a Wildcat, for an average of 12 per game, which ranks him fourth among career leaders in that category. A two-time All-American at UK, he went on to play five years of professional basketball in North America, including stints with the Akron Goodyear Wingfoots of the National Industrial Basketball League, the Cleveland Pipers of the American Basketball League, and the Chicago Zephyrs of the NBA. Cox lives in Hazard.

Johnny Cox earned All-American honors following the 1956–1957 and 1958–1959 basketball seasons. (Courtesy of the University of Kentucky Archives.)

Growing up I didn't know too much about UK basketball because I had never seen the team play. The games weren't televised in the early 1950s. Plus, living in the Appalachian Mountains of Eastern Kentucky, I felt sort of isolated from everything because traveling on the roads at that time was so dangerous. As a result, most people in the mountain communities didn't migrate too far from where they lived. For example, the distance between Hazard and Lexington is about 140 miles, but that trip would take you four hours because the roads were so bad. Since the roadways were upgraded that same trip now takes about one hour and forty-five minutes.

The main support I had came from my parents, Bill and Lula Mae Cox. As a son I wanted to please them. They didn't know much about basketball, but they supported my interest in it.

My high school basketball coach, Goebel Ritter, taught me how to play the game and really brought me along. He coached me a total of three years, first as a freshman at Fleming Neon High School in Neon, Kentucky, and later when I transferred to Hazard High School, where I played during my senior year. Coach Ritter was a disciplinarian. He expected you to do what you were supposed to do. I also did a lot of practicing on my own. That's all I did was play basketball night and day.

I had no idea how good I could be as a player because nobody ever told me. I had to figure it out on my own, so I practiced and played. Back then most high schools in the mountains of Eastern Kentucky had good basketball teams. That made me a better player and helped me learn more about the game. I put a lot of effort into it.

When I was a senior at Hazard High School we competed in the 1955 state high school championship basketball game and won. That game was played in Memorial Coliseum. That brought recognition my way. Because of my success I was offered scholarships from a number of schools, including UK, Eastern Kentucky University, Western Kentucky University, Morehead State University, and the University of Miami in Florida.

Assistant Coach Harry Lancaster was the main person from UK who recruited me. I don't remember feeling pressure from him. He let me make up my own mind. I decided to sign with UK because I felt comfortable there. When I was younger I had visited Lexington twice to watch UK football games, and I remember walking around the university campus and checking out the facilities. In my mind that's where I wanted to be; it was familiar to me.

Coach Adolph Rupp and Coach Lancaster were well organized. If you didn't work hard you didn't do much playing, or you didn't stay with the program. It was pretty much you work, or you leave. I had no reason to leave because that's where I wanted to play. When I wasn't playing basketball I was doing construction work during the summers, so I was used to hard work. It all depends on where you come from and what you're used to.

Coach Rupp and Coach Lancaster didn't really socialize with players outside of basketball. That's the way they ran their program. It was all business. Some of my predecessors who played for UK got into difficulty fooling with other people outside of the basketball program. That always stuck in my mind, so I didn't get involved with people outside of my own circle of friends. I played basketball and attended classes. I minded my own business. But I've made a lot of friends from UK basketball and continue to do so.

When my jersey was retired in the rafters of Rupp Arena I remember feeling like I'd done something worthwhile. I suppose I was successful in basketball at UK because I spent a lot of time fooling with the game, kept trying to get better. When you spend a lot of time doing something, and you don't deviate from it, you get results. It's like working any kind of a job. If you stay on the job a long time, you learn something and get better at it. Basketball is the same way. You become a better player if you stay with it. We had good teams when I was at UK. We put a lot of time into it and a lot of hard work. It was a good experience for me.

Part II

The 1960s–1970s

No other player made his mark on the UK program in the early 1960s like Charles ("Cotton") Nash. The forward led the Wildcats in scoring during his sophomore, junior, and senior seasons and tallied 1,000 points after playing just forty-five games, which remains a school record. He ended his career in 1964 with 1,770 points. Nash was followed by star Wildcat guards Louis Dampier and Pat Riley, who were members of the "Rupp's Runts" squad that fell to Texas Western 72–65 in the NCAA National Championship game on March 19, 1966, a matchup that was the subject of a 2006 film by Disney entitled *Glory Road*.

The late 1960s were marked by two important breakthroughs. On February 18, 1967, Adolph Rupp earned his 760th win, becoming college basketball's all-time winningest coach, when the Wildcats defeated Mississippi State 103–74. Meanwhile, on January 18, 1969, UK became the first program in college basketball history to record 1,000 wins, with a 69–66 victory over SEC rival Tennessee. Center Dan Issel ushered in the 1970s by establishing another milestone. During UK's 90–86 win over Vanderbilt University on February 28, 1970, he became the first Wildcat to score 2,000 points.

The following month he ended his career with 2,138 points, a school record that remains unsurpassed.

After forty-two years at the helm Adolph Rupp retired from coaching at the close of the 1971–1972 campaign. He was seventy years old. Longtime assistant and former UK player Joe B. Hall, a native of Cynthiana, Kentucky, succeeded Rupp. Coach Hall didn't waste any time picking up where his former boss had left off. During his first season as head coach the Wildcats finished with a 22–8 record, including an SEC Championship.

UK began the 1976–1977 season on a new home court in Rupp Arena, a twenty-three-thousand-seat facility in downtown Lexington that accommodated twice as many fans as Memorial Coliseum did and cost $53 million to build. Early in the course of UK's following season Adolph Rupp passed away, on December 10, 1977. Coincidentally, that night number-one-ranked UK defeated Kansas—Rupp's alma mater—in Allen Fieldhouse in Lawrence, Kansas, an arena named after his mentor and former coach, Dr. Forrest C. ("Phog") Allen. The 1977–1978 Wildcats finished the regular season with a 25–2 record and a number-one national ranking going into NCAA Tournament play. Led by a forty-one-point performance by forward and team captain Jack ("Goose") Givens, UK won its fifth NCAA Championship with a 94–88 win over Duke University on March 27, 1978.

8

Charles ("Cotton") Nash

Forward Charles ("Cotton") Nash scored 1,770 points during his three-year varsity career, ranking him ninth on the list of the program's all-time leading scorers. He also ranks second in career double-doubles (forty-four times) and 30-point games (twenty-one times), and during each of his three season he led the Wildcats in scoring (an average of 23.4, 20.6, and 24.0 points per game as a sophomore, junior, and senior, respectively) and rebounding (an average of 13.2, 12.0, and 11.7 rebounds per game as a sophomore, junior, and senior, respectively). He graced the cover of Sports Illustrated *on December 10, 1962.*

Following his UK career Nash played for the NBA's Los Angeles Lakers and the San Francisco Warriors during the 1964–1965 season, but he enjoyed more success later playing for the ABA's Kentucky Colonels, averaging 8.5 points and 4.9 rebounds per game during the 1967–1968 campaign.

A gifted baseball player at UK, Nash played for Major League Baseball's Chicago White Sox and Minnesota Twins between 1967 and 1970 before launching careers in investment and real estate.

Nash and his wife, Julie, have three children, Patrick, J. Richey,

Charles ("Cotton") Nash (right) and Adolph Rupp kneel behind the four NCAA Championship trophies UK won during Rupp's tenure. (Courtesy of the University of Kentucky Archives.)

and Audrey, and seven grandchildren. The couple lives in Lexington, where they breed and race Standardbred horses, a venture they began with Nash's sister, Francene, and other close friends.

UK's assistant basketball coach Harry Lancaster was definitely an influence on me. He groomed all of the freshmen for what to expect. He was the freshman coach, and he prepared everybody for Adolph Rupp in their varsity careers. He was an advisor, a good coach, and he seemed like a friend, more so than Adolph Rupp. He played good cop, bad cop, so to speak, with some of the players.

Coach Lancaster taught us how to interact with the fans, the autograph seekers, and how to handle ourselves in the public spotlight. We were fresh out of high school and had no idea the impact that playing at the UK basketball program would have on us, and the impact it had on not only people in Lexington but people across the state. Coach Lancaster gave us the impression that he was there for us if we needed any help getting acclimated to college life and to big-league basketball. He made us comfortable in that regard. He was also instrumental in recruiting me. I was living in Louisiana at the time, and he paid a couple of recruiting visits to me there when I was still in high school.

Before I signed with UK I made a recruiting visit to Lexington with my family. We toured the campus and looked over the city and were very impressed with it. I was impressed with the whole atmosphere and with Memorial Coliseum, which seated twelve thousand for basketball games and was an enormous gym in those days. The main reason I signed with UK was that I wanted to play college basketball, and I felt like the Southeastern Conference was the conference to go in. I had a chance to play in the Big Ten, the Atlantic Coast Conference, and on the West Coast, but I narrowed it down to the SEC. If you were going to play basketball at that time the premiere program was UK. It still is. That's how I made my decision.

My relationship with Coach Adolph Rupp was all business and on a professional level. I really liked the way he conducted practice. There was no conditioning work because Coach Rupp had practices so drawn up that we were in motion during most every minute, either doing a drill or scrimmaging or shooting. We started practice at exactly 3:15 p.m. and were off the court at 5:00 p.m. We started each practice with a thirty-minute period of free shooting, where you'd shoot the ball, get your own rebound, and come back out and shoot again. That gets you in shape. Our teams were noted for wearing other teams down. We were in much better shape than most of the teams we played.

Another influential person to me was Happy Chandler, who was Kentucky's governor at that time. He attended a lot of our games and would come into the dressing room to give us encouragement. Everybody on the team was impressed that the governor showed up for support. That was a big deal for us.

Governor Chandler liked to give hugs. Sometimes he would kiss you! He had a fantastic personality and was a popular figure in Kentucky at that time. They say that if he met a man once he'd remember that person's name. You can imagine how many people he met during his lifetime as governor and later as the commissioner for Major League Baseball.

The UK fans were just as rabid when I was a player as they are now. I used to receive personal cards and letters. Some people would write a poem and send it to me. Others would draw or paint a picture of me and send it my way. Some fans even sent me scrapbooks they compiled of newspaper clippings related to my career.

I was close to my basketball teammates. We had a communal bond, but three or four of us at the time also played baseball, so we reported to the baseball team right after the basketball season ended.

During the summer months the UK basketball players went their separate ways, it seemed, and we didn't see the basketball coaches until October 15, when the official practice period started, unless you had some academic problems they wanted to discuss with you or give you some suggestions as to how to improve your game. It was a different atmosphere then. There was no emphasis on being involved in the sport year-round as it is today, where the coaches want their athletes to be doing something in regard to basketball year-round.

When I look back on my athletic career I'm fond of the fact that I was able to play in both the National Basketball Association and in Major League Baseball. I think there were only about ten of us in history who did that, including Ronald Lee Reed, Kevin Joseph ("Chuck") Connors, Bill Sharman, and Dick Groat. Gene Conley probably had the best career in both leagues, and Danny Ainge is probably the last athlete to have played in both leagues. That kind of dual career wouldn't be possible today because the NBA and MLB seasons overlap too much, but at that time it was possible.

Another Kentuckian who made an impact on me was Ralph Smith, a former county judge from Western Kentucky who invited me to go to a Standardbred auction with him in the winter of 1989. Ralph and I were friends, and he intended to buy a few horses that day. I had enjoyed watching Standardbreds race at the Red Mile since my college days, but I had never been involved in the business side of it. We sat in the stands and watched the auction go through, and by the time I got home that night I owned part of two horses! Ever since that day my wife and I have been a part of the Standardbred business, mainly breeding and racing horses. We go to the yearling sale each year and pick out a couple of good-looking yearlings to raise. We concentrate on fillies most years, so when their racing days are over we can move them into the breeding shed and have a secondary career for them. That was our strategy when we started, and we're still trying to adhere to that. I almost feel like I'm a coach and the horses are my players.

In the fall of 2011 a local merchant asked me to come by and sign autographs on a Saturday afternoon. I was only committed for two hours, but there was a steady stream of people well beyond that time frame. That was amazing to me after being removed from the program since 1964.

I chose to settle in Kentucky because I married a girl from Mount Sterling—Julie Richey, whom I met at UK—and her parents lived in the state. In the off-season we'd rent an apartment in Lexington, and we finally decided to buy a home and live here permanently. I thought it was a great place to raise children—a great area and a great town. It still is.

9

Larry Conley

Ashland, Kentucky, native Larry Conley was a key member of the Ashland High School Tomcats basketball team that won a state championship in 1961 and finished in the runner-up spot in 1962, his senior season.

At UK, Conley led the Wildcats in assists as a sophomore, junior, and senior, and he ranks ninth all-time in assists per game among players who competed in at least sixty games (an average of 3.62 per game). He scored ten points and grabbed eight rebounds in UK's 72–65 loss to Texas Western in the 1966 NCAA National Championship game in College Park, Maryland.

After a ten-year stint as a salesman and promotional representative for Converse shoes, Conley started broadcasting college basketball games in 1979 for ESPN, a role he currently holds with Fox Sports Network. To date he has called games for more than 230 NCAA college basketball teams.

Conley lives in Dunwoody, Georgia, with his wife, Lorie. The couple has two grown sons.

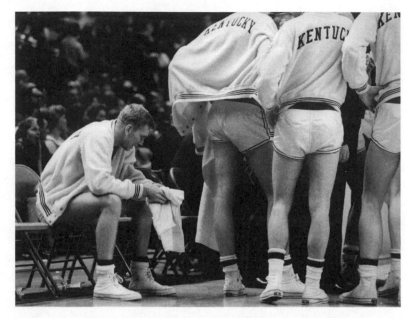

Larry Conley (left) on the bench after fouling out during the 1966 NCAA Championship game against Texas Western. (Courtesy of the University of Kentucky Archives.)

I grew up in Ashland, Kentucky, with my ears tuned in to a small transistor radio, listening to UK games at night, with Claude Sullivan or Cawood Ledford calling the action. A lot of former UK players don't have that kind of attachment, but when you grow up in a state with something as popular as UK basketball is, if you're a dyed-in-the-wool fan, and if you were a really good player, UK was the number-one place to consider, because you wanted to be a part of that storied tradition. The history of Kentucky basketball had an impact on me more than anything. In conjunction with that was the presence of Coach Adolph Rupp, who started the winning tradition at UK.

On the court, Coach Rupp and Assistant Coach Harry Lancaster had a profound effect on me, but in different ways. Coach Rupp had a "bigger than life" aura about him. He macromanaged UK basketball, while Coach Lancaster micromanaged it. If something was going on wrong in a game and we took a time out, Coach Rupp would spend thirty seconds blistering everybody for not doing what they were supposed to be doing. Coach Lancaster would spend the rest of the time out going into the minutiae. He would say, "Here's what's not happening. Here's what needs to happen." They were a great team together.

The arrival of Joe B. Hall as an assistant coach at the start of my senior year was also influential. I give Coach Hall a lot of credit for enabling our team to reach the NCAA National Championship in 1966, because he brought in a conditioning program and a new look to the program. I think it's something Coach Rupp needed at that point in time. Coach Hall brought a greater respect for the number-three coaching spot on the staff. Before he arrived, most players called coaches other than Coach Rupp and Coach Lancaster by their first names. But Coach Hall was different. He arrived having served as head coach at Regis College in Denver. One day we were getting ready to go out for the conditioning program. I turned to him and said, "Joe, listen . . ." He stopped me right there and said, "Don't you ever call me Joe. I am Coach Hall."

I looked at him and said, "Yes, sir." That type of respect was important to him, and it carried a lot of weight.

Tom Kron, my former UK teammate, was my very best friend in all of my life. He died from cancer in 2007. After we left UK we stayed in touch and spoke almost weekly. He was almost like a brother to me. I miss him.

During my time at UK I had about a half-dozen professors that I thought were really good teachers. The best professor I had was Herb Drennon, who taught a course in world politics. He was a terrific teacher; the way he would interweave personal stories along with material from the class textbook was remarkable. There were times Professor Drennon would say, "Put your pencils down. Let me tell you a story." How many professors do that? I was excited to go to his class. I truly couldn't wait to get there, because it was so interesting to me. To this day I closely follow politics nationally and around the world, principally because of what he taught me.

One summer I took a terrific class from Don Ivey, a professor who taught classical music. He was so passionate about classical music, and it showed. That was an enjoyable class. To this day I when I get settled in my office, if I'm not listening to country music, I'm listening to classical music. I took classes at UK every summer, not because my grades were bad but because I wanted to graduate in four years. I didn't want to hang around any longer than that.

I'm probably known more for a game I lost than for any game I ever won. I'm speaking about the game we played against Texas Western University for the 1966 NCAA National Championship, which we lost 72–65. It was one of those nights where things went all wrong for us and went right for Texas Western. I don't take anything away from their team; they were a solid club that played a terrific defense against us. Some people want to make something racial out of that game because all five starters on Texas Western were black and all of our starters were white. For those of us who played in that game—and I mean players on both teams—that was the last thing on our minds. It was inconsequential to playing for a national championship. That was certainly not the first time UK had matched up against a team with black players. In my opinion the media took that game and ran with it.

What I remember most about that game against Texas Western was the fact that Pat Riley, who was terrific all season long, had the worst shooting night he'd had all season. He just couldn't make a basket. We prepared ourselves well on the defensive end to handle them, but they were much more patient offensively than we were. They controlled the ball movement. Back then there was no shot clock, so they took their time and worked the ball around and got it to the right position. I credit their coach, Don Haskins, for preparing them really well.

Playing at a high-exposure program like UK puts you out in front of a lot of people. I think you learn to handle yourself well. If you don't, it becomes obvious, and you melt back into the shadows. I think that had a great deal of effect on me. It gives you confidence, because you know that people are interested in what you have to say and in what you're doing.

10

Dan Issel

Former UK center Dan Issel racked up 2,138 points between 1967 and 1970, ranking him as the program's all-time leading scorer (an average of 25.8 per game). He is also the program's career leader in rebounds (1,078, or an average of 13 per game) and field goals made in a single season (369 during the 1969–1970 campaign), and he ranks second, behind Kenny Walker, in career free throws made (550). For thirty-nine years he held the school record for most points in a single game (53), before guard Jodie Meeks inched him out with a 54-point shooting performance in a win over Tennessee on January 13, 2009.

After his UK career Issel signed with the Kentucky Colonels of the ABA and was named the league's rookie of the year in 1971, averaging 29.9 points per game. He won the 1975 ABA Championship with the Colonels and spent the last ten seasons of his career playing for the Denver Nuggets of the NBA, where he finished his career averaging 20.7 points per game.

After Issel retired from the NBA in 1985 he received the league's J. Walter Kennedy Citizenship Award for outstanding service to the Denver community. He was elected to the Naismith Memorial Basketball Hall of Fame in 1993.

Dan Issel (44) scored fifty-three points against Ole Miss on February 7, 1970, a school record he held for thirty-nine years. Here, he puts up a shot against Vanderbilt in 1969. (Courtesy of the University of Kentucky Archives.)

Today Issel resides in Windsor, Colorado, with his wife, Cheri. The couple has two children, Sheridan and Scott; three grandsons, Benjamin, Brody, and Greyson; and one granddaughter, Addison.

Very good memories come to mind when I think of Kentucky. I have told people that I was blessed to have played fifteen years of professional basketball, but as I look back on my career, my four years at UK were the best that I had. That's why I hate to see some of today's young players leave college early for careers in the NBA.

I understand that the opportunity to earn a significant income in the NBA is appealing, but four years of college was a very innocent and enjoyable time for me. Once I got to the pros it was all about basketball, but my college experience was more diverse. At UK, I had basketball, which was more important and revered than I expected, but also the experience of attending classes, the beauty of the campus, and the beauty of Central Kentucky. I was fortunate to meet my wife, Cheri, at UK; she was a cheerleader at the university. We married in 1969.

A few people in particular had an influence on me during my career at UK. One was Coach Rupp. You don't find many people who are lukewarm on Coach Rupp. They either loved playing for him or they hated playing for him, for a couple of reasons. Today, you have to coach the individual; you have to understand which player you have to pat on the back to motivate and which player you have to kind of kick in the pants to motivate. Coach Rupp's philosophy was that you kicked everybody in the pants, and if you weren't strong enough to take it, he didn't want you on his team. I blossomed in that system because I grew up on a farm, and I had a good work ethic. My mentality was *I'm going to prove to you that I'm going to work hard enough be successful.* So Coach Rupp's philosophy of coaching was suited perfectly for my personality. He was tough, but he was fair. I got to know him a little better than a lot of his players did because he retired in 1972 and had a relationship with the Kentucky Colonels of the ABA while I was playing there. We also launched a basketball camp together with my former teammate Mike Pratt called the Rupp-Issel-Pratt Basketball Camp. That camp took place at Centre College in Danville for a couple of years and then moved to Bellarmine University in Louisville.

I really grew to appreciate Coach Rupp. He was an amazing man. Here was a guy who never made more than twenty thousand dollars a year when he was coaching at UK, but when he passed away his estate was worth millions of dollars. He had a strong work ethic, and he influenced me a great deal, the notion of being able to accomplish something if you worked hard enough at it. To this day, in my wallet I carry a typewritten quote from Theodore Roosevelt that Coach Rupp was fond of and often quoted. It reads: *It is not the critic who counts; not the man who points out how the strong man stumbles, or where the doer of deeds could have done them better. The credit belongs to the man who is actually in the arena, whose face is marred by dust and sweat and blood; who strives valiantly; who errs, and comes short again and again, because there is no effort without error and shortcoming; but who does actually strive to do the deeds; who knows the great enthusiasms, the great devotions; who spends himself in a worthy cause; who at the best knows in the end the triumph of high achievement, and who at the worst, if he fails, at least fails while daring greatly, so that his place shall never be with those cold and timid souls who know neither victory nor defeat.*[1]

In a nutshell, that was Coach Rupp's philosophy.

During my senior year Mike Pratt and I served as team captains. From the time classes started at the end of August to the fifteenth of October we had a very difficult six-week running program led by Assistant Coach Joe B. Hall. At the beginning of that year our teammates called a meeting and asked us to approach Coach Rupp to see if he could soften that running program a little bit. Mike and I went into Coach Rupp's office, and we said something to the effect of, "This isn't our idea. We're here as representatives of the team, but the guys think that program is a little tough and wonder if we could cut it back a little bit."

I don't remember how Mike was excused from that meeting, but I eventually found myself in Coach Rupp's office all by myself, and he never addressed the running program. He said to me, "Do you realize you have a chance to become the all-time leading scorer at Kentucky?"

"Well, I know with a good senior year that would be possible," I replied.

"You go out there and run today, and I'll do everything I can to see that you get that record," he said.

There were only six of us in the running program: five freshmen and me. The next day everybody was back out at the track, and the running program didn't get any easier. In fact, it got a little harder. But Coach Rupp kept his word. He kept me in some games that season well after the game was decided. Basketball is a team sport, so individual records don't mean very much, but since 1970 I've held the scoring record for the men's basketball program at UK. Coach Rupp had an awful lot to do with that.

The other people who influenced me during my days as a player were the Lexington couple Armand ("Mondo") and Joyce Angelucci.[2] Mondo's father started a clothing store on Main Street called Angelucci's. One of his brothers ran the clothing store. Mondo was an attorney and later became a judge in Kentucky. I was terribly homesick when I first arrived in Lexington from my hometown of Batavia, Illinois. The UK Athletics Department "assigned" Mondo and Joyce to me to look out for my well-being.

I would spend almost every Sunday afternoon at their house in Lexington, especially during the NFL season to watch football, but

I was also welcome at their house when I got tired of hanging out at the dorm. I didn't like the dorm life.

There were some times I got so homesick during my freshman year that I came close to pulling up stakes and going home to Illinois. Mondo and Joyce got me through those times, not only with their advice but with their love and offering that home setting. Not every player who went to UK needed or took advantage of that support, but it was really important to me.

I would go over to the Angeluccis' house every Tuesday night to watch *The Fugitive,* which at the time was the highest-rated television show ever. That was something special we shared. My mom and dad happened to be in town the day they aired the final episode of that show in August 1967. We went out to dinner around 4:30 that afternoon so we could be back at Joyce and Mondo's house to watch that final episode.

Mondo was a great friend and great mentor. Whenever I had a problem or needed someone to talk to while I was at UK, he was the one that would listen. In fact, he negotiated my first professional contract when I signed with the Kentucky Colonels.

It's difficult for non-Kentucky natives or those who don't live in the state to understand how important basketball is to Kentuckians. The passion is impossible to describe. During my nine seasons playing for the Denver Nuggets, I witnessed "Broncomania" (fan devotion to the National Football League's Denver Broncos team) firsthand. It's huge, because the Broncos were that state's first professional team. Colorado residents love the Broncos, win or lose, but their passion doesn't come close to what the fan base of UK feels about their basketball program. In most American communities, conversation struck up in a grocery store revolves around the weather or politics. In Kentucky, you talk about Kentucky basketball; it doesn't matter if it's during the season or in the middle of the summer. That's what you talk about.

What's most amazing to me is that I graduated from UK in 1970, but I can walk down the street in Lexington, and people will speak to me like I played yesterday. This is what has so blessed me. The loyalty of the UK fan to that basketball program is unmatched.

I remember how much fans supported us at road games. We'd play at the University of Mississippi and at Mississippi State University, and there would be as many Kentucky fans at those games as there would be for the home team. A lot of those UK fans couldn't get tickets to games at Memorial Coliseum, so they'd book trips to some of the Southeastern Conference away games.

By car, it was 420 miles one way to Lexington from my hometown in Illinois. My mom and dad only missed three home games over the span of my UK career. They'd always bring my sister and brother, or another couple, but sometimes I needed more than the four seats we were allotted. Before nearly every home game I'd walk into Coach Rupp's office and say, "Coach, I need two extra tickets for the game."

"Son, do you know how much those tickets are worth?"

"Yes, sir," I'd say. "But they're for family."

"I don't think I'll have any, but if I do I'll put them in your locker on game night."

Those tickets were always there, but Coach Rupp sure enjoyed teasing me.

Getting tickets for friends, however, wasn't so easy. Mike Casey, Mike Pratt, and I always had buddies who wanted to come to home games. Hours before game time we'd let a few of them into Memorial Coliseum. We had a duplicate key made for a lock that secured one of the back doors to the coliseum, and our buddies would hide in the wooden phone booths that were located on the concourse level until the game started.

The only reason I went to the ABA after my UK career as opposed to the NBA was because I was offered an opportunity to stay in Kentucky and play for the Kentucky fans as a member of the Kentucky Colonels. After playing in the ABA and having a chance to develop, I was able to go on and play ten years in the NBA. I'm not so sure that if I had gone directly from UK to the NBA that I would have had the success in basketball that I wound up having. That's how significantly the Kentucky fans impacted me.

My career playing for UK also exposed me to the Thoroughbred industry, which I grew to love. In fact, the first thing I bought when I signed my first professional contract was a broodmare. I had a partnership with Tom Gentry, who was a flamboyant horseman in Lexington.

I credit Tom for cultivating my love for the Thoroughbred industry. He took me on my first-ever visit to Keeneland during my freshman year, and during summers I'd work Keeneland horse sales events with him. A lot of people didn't like Tom. They thought he was a showoff and pushy. He was to a certain extent, but he was a pioneer in marketing the horses he had to sell.

If you go to a Keeneland horse sale today, everything you see around the barn area was the brainchild of Tom Gentry, from the barn signs and the flowers to the giveaways and the snacks to the ink pens. To be around that when I was a young was a lot of fun, and we became partners owning horses after my playing days at UK.

Tom and I had horses together for years. I like everything about the industry. Some people are just attracted to the racing and to the betting, but I like going to the horse farms and watching the foals. There's a correlation, I think, between Thoroughbred racehorses and professional athletes. That is, you can breed the very top mare to the very top stallion, but that's no guarantee that horse will excel at racing, because you don't know how competitive they are; you don't know what's in their heart. It's the same thing with athletes. You can overcome a lot of physical deficiencies if you're willing to work hard and see how big your heart is.

11

Joe B. Hall

Cynthiana, Kentucky, native Joe B. Hall played varsity basketball at UK during the 1948–1949 campaign before transferring to the University of the South in Sewanee, Tennessee. In 1956 he began his coaching career at Kentucky's Shepherdsville High School, followed by a five-year head coaching stint at Regis College in Denver and a one-year head coaching assignment at Central Missouri State in Warrensburg. In 1965 he accepted an offer from Adolph Rupp to become an assistant coach at UK.

Hall succeeded Rupp as head coach in 1973 and guided the 1978 squad to UK's fifth NCAA National Championship. During his thirteen-year tenure he guided the Wildcats to eight Southeastern Conference titles and one SEC Tournament championship. He was named the National Coach of the Year in 1978, was named the SEC Coach of the Year four times, and was inducted into the National Collegiate Basketball Hall of Fame in 2012.

Hall was married to his wife, Katharine, for fifty-five years before she passed away in 2007. The couple had three children, Judy, Kathy, and Steve, and three grandchildren, Jeffrey, Laura, and Katharine.

Hall currently cohosts a sports radio talk show with former Uni-

During Joe B. Hall's thirteen-year coaching tenure, twenty-three former UK players were drafted by the NBA, including five in the first round. (Courtesy of the University of Kentucky Archives.)

versity of Louisville men's basketball coach Denny Crum called The Joe B. and Denny Show. *He lives in Lexington.*

I was mentored by a lot of fine Kentuckians at an early age. Larkie Box was a former marine who came out of the service to work with the junior varsity basketball team in my hometown of Cynthiana, Kentucky. I looked up to him because of his war service and his past athletic success. He had been a star basketball player at Cynthiana High School when I was a little kid. He inspired me and mentored me in just about everything: not only in sports but life in general. He even taught me how to drive a car.

Coach Box used to have access to horses. One day he showed up at the local community youth center downtown and said he'd take me home. He had this big old fat-bellied horse with no saddle, so we both got on him. The streets back then used to be arched in the middle. The horse began to run up the street toward my house, and the feet slipped out from under him, and Coach Box and I fell off. The horse landed partially on us, and we slid on the asphalt pavement. The horse got up and ran, but we were too crippled to get up; we just crawled to the gutter to get out of the way. We were both laughing. Coach Box was so good to me, and he made athletics fun.

My high school basketball coach, Kelly Stanfield, was another mentor. There never was a finer gentleman and one who contributed to all phases of my development, such as how to be a good citizen and sportsmanship. He instilled those principles in me at a very early age. He would praise my defense and put me on the best opponent during games. He talked me up so much I felt like I had to give a superhuman effort. Kelly Stanfield coached for many years, and I don't think he lost more than five games in any one season. He later became principal of Cynthiana High School.

My high school football coach, Bill Boswell, also took a special interest in me. I was the only freshman on the varsity football team, and that year he bought me a book on how to quarterback—how to call plays in certain situations, what not to do, and how to control the huddle. He groomed me to be a quarterback. In fact, I played quarterback my last three years of high school, and I was captain of both the football and basketball teams. I'm in the Cynthiana High School Football Hall of Fame, which I consider one of my greatest accomplishments; I love that distinction.

Coach Boswell was very mild mannered, but you took everything to heart that he said, because you knew he cared about you. He was also my Sunday school teacher. Later, after I got out of high school, I did some farm work for him. I was running farm-service machinery, and I bailed straw out of straw stacks on his farm.

My father, Charles C. ("Bill") Hall, was also influential. He was a sheriff in Harrison County, so I had to live by the foot of the cross. I remember one night I got home about ten minutes after 10:00 p.m. The curfew set by Coach Stanfield was 10:00 p.m. When I walked in the door my dad was on the phone to Coach Stanfield, telling him I was late. Dad also had my health in mind. A lot of the kids smoked back then. My dad told me that I could smoke if I wanted to, but if I smoked I couldn't play sports. So I never smoked a cigarette.

As I grew older, other men who became influential were Coach Lon Varnell,[1] Coach Hank Iba,[2] and, of course, Coach Adolph Rupp, whom I played for and spent seven years as his assistant coach. I had a strange relationship with Coach Rupp. He recruited me to play guard at UK and gave me a scholarship. But after I played one year on the varsity squad, I realized that we had so many guards that I wasn't going to be a factor on the team, so I talked to Coach Rupp about transferring to another school. He got on the phone immediately, called me back the next morning, and had two scholarship offers for me: one to Duke University and one to Xavier University. At the same time, I heard Lon Varnell, basketball coach at the University of the South in Sewanee, Tennessee, on the radio saying he was in Kentucky looking for a guard, someone who could play immediately. I called Coach Rupp. He happened to know Coach Varnell very well, so he called him, called me back, and set up my transfer to Sewanee.

After my playing days at the University of the South I started my college coaching career at Regis College in Denver, followed by Central Missouri State. I was coaching at Central Missouri State when Coach Rupp called to ask if I would be his assistant coach back at UK. What a great compliment he paid me with that offer, and I worked very hard for him. I couldn't help him as a player for UK, but I had the opportunity to help him win six Southeastern Conference championships in the last seven years of his coaching career. Three years before he retired, Coach Rupp recommended that I be his successor. I appreciate so much what he did for me and the opportunity he gave me.

My wife, Katharine, was also a tremendous influence on me. She could have written a book on how to be a coach's wife. She was supportive and understanding of the demands on me that took so much of my time, being out late at night recruiting and so on. I'd come into the Lexington airport, and she'd bring me a fresh suitcase full of clothes and take my dirty clothes back to get them ready for another trip. She had so much more of the responsibility of running the house and raising our kids than I did, with me gone so much. Once, early in my coaching career, I had to be out of town overnight. It was the middle of winter, and the furnace in our house died. She had to get a serviceman out to fix the furnace before our kids froze.

Katharine was like a mom to the UK players and loved cooking for them especially. We had players come to our home, and she would take care of them when they had a tooth pulled or had some kind of illness. Once, our whole team got sick two or three days before a game. Katharine organized the boosters to cook enough chicken noodle soup to feed them until they got back on their feet.

I gained a good understanding of the UK fan base when I was Coach Rupp's assistant. As I recruited all over the state and as I traveled for various speaking engagements, the buzz was all about UK basketball. Of course, the University of Louisville Cardinals had a big following, but mostly it was confined to Jefferson County and not too much in other parts of the state. Each smaller state school had its own following, but their fans also followed UK. The early success of Coach Rupp and his four NCAA National Championship wins that spanned over two decades really built the tradition at UK.

When he retired, Coach Rupp said that he left a program that was built on a solid foundation, one that would carry itself for years to come. He was right. The fan support in this state is unequaled anywhere. I say that knowing the following that Duke University, the University of North Carolina, UCLA, and the University of Notre Dame have. They have other pretenders in their back door that Kentucky doesn't have. Kentucky is the Commonwealth's team, and the support goes border to border.

The fan devotion of Big Blue Nation was a stimulus to my hard work. I knew what was expected from the fans and knew that if I didn't do my job, I wasn't going to be here for very long. I recruited hard and did what I had to do to coach up my teams. I was very serious about what it meant to so many people. I tried not to let those fans down. The pressure was there, but there was also opportunity. When you have tradition like UK's you don't have any trouble talking to a recruit.

Five coaches—Coach Rupp, me, Rick Pitino, Tubby Smith, and John Calipari—have won national championships in this atmosphere. There is no other college or university that has more than three coaches who have won national championships for their institution. What does that tell you? It tells you a lot about tradition. It tells you about fans and expectations that stimulate the administration to give you the support to hire the right people who can win.

The fan devotion is incredible, from people who go to all kinds of extremes to come to games to people who line up out outside of the arena days before a scrimmage to get tickets. When your players witness that kind of interest, they become serious and focused. When they know it's so important to so many people, they start grasping what their responsibility is. You don't have to tell them. They can feel it. When you put demands on them in terms of preseason conditioning, hitting the weight room, and giving them instructions, they're ready to listen to you. They take coaching seriously, and they know the importance of what they're doing. That's a great tool for a coach to have. Expectation of the fans is an enormous stimulus to their focus.

UK fans place their head basketball coach on a pedestal because that person is the leader of what they love so much. It's a rock star effect for the players and everybody associated with the program. In my case, I never dreamed of having an opportunity to play basketball at UK, let alone becoming the head coach. Growing up, I had so much respect for the players and what they accomplished; I never even pictured myself in that role. When I did earn a basketball scholarship and walked out on to the court to represent the university, I was still in awe.

When I became the head coach, it wasn't a dream come true, because I had never dreamed that the opportunity would present itself to me. I always held the head coaching job at UK in such high regard because I had so much respect for Coach Rupp. Even to be criticized in comparison to him was an honor. I never tried to remove his shadow from the program. I didn't try to fill his shoes.

I just tried to do the best I could. I didn't expect anything more. It was a humbling experience for me to have the honor of being associated with the program that I loved for so long.

I'm the only native Kentuckian to ever coach at UK, at least since the tenure of Coach Rupp, who was from Kansas. I'm a native son who had the opportunity to do something that I dearly believed in and loved.

12

Mike Pratt

Former forward Mike Pratt led the 1967–1968 UK squad in assists, averaging 3.5 per game that season. He tallied twenty-nine double-doubles between 1968 and 1970, ranking him eighth among the program's career leaders in that category. He finished his career with 1,359 points, which ranks him twenty-sixth among all-time players.

As a Wildcat Pratt earned All-SEC honors twice, was a second-team Converse All-American in 1970, Kentucky's third Academic All-American, and a two-time Academic All-SEC selection.

After his UK career he played two seasons for the American Basketball Association's Kentucky Colonels and then joined the coaching ranks, first as an assistant coach and then as head coach at the University of North Carolina, Charlotte. He later served as an assistant coach for the National Basketball Association's Charlotte Hornets.

Pratt works and lives in Louisville and is a broadcast analyst for Wildcats basketball games on the UK Radio Network.

Forward Mike Pratt scored forty-two points against Notre Dame on December 27, 1969. Here he dribbles by an Auburn defender. (Courtesy of Mike Pratt.)

I was born in Dayton, Ohio, but I feel like I'm an adopted son of Kentucky. My teammate Mike Casey, who was also my roommate at UK, was born and raised in Shelbyville and was a high school basketball hero there. I met a lot of Kentuckians through him and others through additional teammates who were from Kentucky. In fact, seven guys on our freshman team were natives. They were my guiding light for information on Kentucky and its basketball history, and they shared in their own way what it meant to them to be at the University of Kentucky on a basketball scholarship.

These guys knew so much about different schools and players around the state because they had played against many of them during their high school careers and in the annual Kentucky Boys' State Basketball Tournament, which is a huge event in the Commonwealth.

As players for UK we lived in a glass bowl, but it was a much smaller glass bowl than the one today's players live in. Everything is relative. We'd often get mail from people wanting autographs. People would send letters to the Athletic Department, and they'd pass them down to us. Or, if we went out somewhere in Lexington, we were recognized very quickly, which was a big thrill. After a while it could get old, but early on it was a big thrill. People always were very nice.

We used to sell out games at Memorial Coliseum. We even had sellout crowds for freshman games! The first time I realized how important basketball was to Kentuckians was during my freshman year, when we traveled to Louisville to play at Freedom Hall. The varsity team went out and practiced, and then our freshman team went out and practiced—a shoot-around. There were twelve thousand people there to watch that day's shoot-around. I remember thinking, "Wow. This is special." That was my first indication of what the UK fan base stood for and how closely they followed the basketball team.

Throughout my whole career there would be twelve to four-teen thousand people just to watch an hour of practice. Of course, the fans got in for free, and there were no televised broadcasts of the practices, like there are today from time to time.

There were two main reasons I decided to play for the University of Kentucky instead of for other schools. First, UK had a great team my senior year of high school: Rupp's Runts (the 1965–1966 squad). I came down from Ohio to watch them play. They won twenty-five games in a row and went to the Final Four, losing to Texas Western in the championship game, so they got a lot of publicity. There were a lot of things written in the newspapers and in *Sports Illustrated* about this team: they were small, they ran, shot, and passed well, all those fundamentals. That team attracted me as far as the style they played and what they showed in terms of team-work. The second key reason I decided to play for Kentucky was that I wanted to go away from home to attend college. If I hadn't wanted to go away from home, I probably would have gone to the University of Dayton or the University of Cincinnati.

Anybody who plays basketball for Kentucky always feels good when they're out in the state and somebody remembers them or rec-ognizes them. That is another reason that the connection between the players and the fans of Big Blue Nation is so unique. If you're on the team and you're a good person and you do the right things, the fans never seem to forget you. They may not recognize you as you get older, but they remember names, because they follow the team so well. That's a great feeling for a former player as you go through life and you get older.

In my case, I have a bit of an advantage because I do play-by-play for games on the UK Radio Network, so I'm around the bas-ketball setting. But even before I started doing radio play-by-play, fans would recognize me. About six years after my career playing for the Kentucky Colonels I spent some time in Charlotte, North Carolina, first as an assistant coach for the University of North Carolina, Charlotte, where I eventually became head coach, then as an assistant coach for the NBA's Charlotte Hornets. In those settings UK fans would come up to me and say, "Mike, I went to the University of Kentucky," or "My brother saw you play," or "You know my brother." There were always multiple people from Kentucky who would come up to me. That was always very interesting.

These days, when Kentucky fans approach me and want to talk about basketball, they often ask about the current team or about certain games I played in, such as what it was like to play against "Pistol Pete" Pete Maravich, or remark about the orange sports coat that former University of Tennessee coach Ray Mears used to wear. During my playing days TV coverage of UK was limited, so fans enjoy when I can "fill in the blanks" for them about certain games. They also enjoy stories about Coach Rupp.

My sophomore year we played in Knoxville, Tennessee, the first of two regular-season games against the University of Tennessee Volunteers. They blew us out, and we were the higher-ranked team. The real story of the game was that the UT students threw oranges at us when we came and left the floor for warm-ups. The press made a big deal of that due to the rivalry between these two schools. Four weeks or so later the Volunteers traveled to Memorial Coliseum in Lexington for a second matchup with us. As the first UT player was introduced, a volley of oranges was thrown by some spectators at the UT bench, followed by another round after the second UT player was introduced. Coach Rupp walked to the middle of the press table, grabbed the microphone, and told the crowd to stop. After he put the microphone down, he winked at our team as he made his way back toward our bench. In the meantime another UT player was introduced, and a new barrage of oranges rained down from the student section. A smile appeared on Coach Rupp's face. We won that game, which was our sixth win in a row after the loss in Knoxville. We continued on to win twelve straight that season before we were beaten on a last-second shot by Ohio State in an NCAA Regional Final.

It never ceases to amaze me when and where I run into UK fans. The Big Blue Nation seems to be everywhere. Now with more television and the Internet and all of the different media that have developed over the past fifteen to twenty years, the base has expanded more than ever. The access to games is easier and greater than ever before. As a result, people follow the team even more than they did back in my day, which is terrific.

Why are UK fans so devoted? Kentucky is a small state. It doesn't have a professional baseball team or a professional football team. For years college basketball has united the state, whether it be at Western Kentucky University, Murray State University, the University of Louisville, or the University of Kentucky—it's the one thing outside of the Kentucky Colonels that has really united this state and the fan base of all the institutions of higher education. I think UK has been the leader in that respect. The other schools have developed their fan base, but UK was the first, won national championships, and they have a following from one side of Kentucky to the other: north, south, east, and west. That's why it's in an enviable position.

I can identify with that kind of devotion because I developed lifelong friends during and after my time at UK. Those friends I've kept in touch with, more so than people I went to high school with in Ohio. When I moved away from Kentucky to coach in North Carolina, I came back to the Bluegrass State because I felt comfortable— just like I felt comfortable playing for the Kentucky Colonels after playing for UK. The people of Kentucky make you feel comfortable.

Sometimes you hear people use the phrase "Boy, I'd like to do something over again," referring to a wish to "do over" some part of their life. I'm not so sure I'd want to do anything about my UK experience over again. I was lucky to get it done the way I got it done. It's been a terrific ride. What more can I say?

13

Kevin Grevey

Forward Kevin Grevey scored 1,801 points during his three varsity seasons with UK, ranking him seventh on the list of all-time leading scorers in the program's history. He had 30-point games eleven times in his career, ranking him fourth in that category, behind Dan Issel, Cotton Nash, and Louis Dampier. As a junior he led the 1972–1973 squad in free-throw percentage, making 83 percent of his shots from the charity stripe, and he ranks third all-time in career scoring, with a 21.4 points per game average.

Grevey's last game as a Wildcat came in the spring of 1975, when UK lost to UCLA in the NCAA National Championship game. He scored thirty-four points in that contest and was named a member of the all–Final Four team.

Three years after he was drafted by the NBA's Washington Bullets, Grevey helped that organization win the 1978 NBA Championship, as part of a team that included Wes Unseld and Elvin Hayes.

Grevey currently lives in Great Falls, Virginia, with his wife, Sandy, and their three children, Amanda, Kevin, and Andrew. They operate a restaurant and sports bar in Falls Church, Virginia, that bears his last name. The couple also runs the Grevey Foundation, a small charity dedicated to helping disadvantaged children in the region.

Kevin Grevey earned first-team All-SEC honors following each of his three seasons at UK and All-American honors following his junior and senior years. (Courtesy of *The Cats' Pause.*)

My hometown of Hamilton, Ohio, is just north of Cincinnati, so it wasn't far away to the border of Kentucky. When I was a boy and our parents drove us across the Ohio River and into in the Bluegrass State, it felt like a completely different place than what I was used to. That set the bar for me at an early age. In fact, when I was about ten years old we took our first family vacation to the Campbell House in Lexington. To stay at a hotel was a big deal at that young age, but my parents didn't have to work hard to get me and my sister out of the hotel pool or out of the room to go take a ride because the area was so beautiful.

We drove around looking at the horse farms and the tobacco farms, and we drove around the UK campus. It was all so new and different to me; I hadn't seen anything like it. We also traveled through the rural areas of the state. My grandparents were from Crab Orchard, Kentucky, so I had some roots and heritage there that I learned to love and respect. When I got older and started dreaming, UK was certainly on my radar as a place I wanted to go to school.

When I think of Kentucky today I think of the fabulous people in that state who are so proud of their southern heritage and who welcomed me when I was a player and made me feel so great. When my wife and kids go back there, they remark, "Boy, this is one special place." I currently live in Great Falls, Virginia, and the nearby towns of Middleburg and Leesburg remind me of Kentucky. That's part of the reason why I love living here in Virginia so much.

I would have never gone to UK if it weren't for Coach Joe B. Hall, who took a personal interest in me and was there for me through the good and the bad. He molded me into a tough, hard-nosed basketball player and a good teammate, I think, because he always emphasized respecting every guy on the team. For example, sometimes a player would sit on the bench for an entire game, but

Coach Hall would give him the game ball at the end of a game because that player may have had a good practice that week, or he may have showed support to his teammates somehow. Looking back, I love that team approach Coach Hall underscored. I learned so much from that.

There was a stretch early in my sophomore year when I had a couple of bad practices in a row. Coach Hall was all over me and everyone else on the team. He was tenacious about making us better and pushing us. One day I missed every open shot I had, didn't get back on defense, the man I was guarding was beating me, and opponents were going over the top of me for rebounds. In my mind, everything I was doing was wrong. I was so angry at myself that I removed myself from practice. I walked off the court and went into the locker room. The first person to come in was the assistant coach Dick Parsons, who said, "Kevin, what's wrong?"

I was crying and in a fragile state of mind.

"Stay here; shake it off," Coach Parsons said. "I want Coach Hall to come and talk to you."

A few minutes later Coach Hall walked in, and he was very compassionate. "Kevin, I love your competitiveness," he said. "You're so hard on yourself, and I can see it, but that's what's going to make you great. That is what's going to make you special. I love how you approach the game, but everyone has bad days."

He then shared a story with me about Pat Riley. "Pat was a player we relied on, and he was so much like you," he said. "He put so much pressure on himself."

Next, Coach Hall asked me to reflect on why I started playing basketball in the first place.

"Because I love basketball," I said.

"There you go," he said. "You've got to have fun and enjoy what you're doing out there on the court, love the game and accept its spoils and rewards. I don't think you're having fun. Take a shower, come back tomorrow, and let's have a better frame of mind. You're putting way too much pressure on yourself."

That's exactly what I needed to hear, because I wasn't having fun. I was miserable because I was putting so much pressure on myself, and I wasn't getting the results from all the effort I was putting in. It just kept mounting. I came back out the next day of practice and broke that rut, and I never looked back.

Years later, when I had my down moments in the NBA—when I was in a shooting slump or when we were in a tough situation, or I wasn't playing to a level I thought I should be playing—I always remembered that conversation with Coach Hall. It was a pivotal moment for me. I needed that positive reinforcement at that time.

Coach Hall also gave me a couple of memorable history lessons about the importance of Kentucky basketball to people in the state. One lesson came on a Southern Airlines charter we took from Mississippi back home to Lexington after a Monday-night game with the Mississippi State University Bulldogs. It was late—eleven at night or so—and Coach Hall called me up to the front of the cabin and asked me to sit in the window seat next to him.

"Look out that window," he said to me. "What do you see down there?"

"I don't see anything," I replied. "It's just black."

He asked the pilot for our whereabouts. We were near the Tennessee-Kentucky border, and soon we'd be flying over Bowling Green, Kentucky. When we reached the vicinity of Bowling Green, Coach Hall turned to me and said, "Look down there now. What do you see?"

"I see a lot of lights on," I said.

"You didn't see any lights on back there over Tennessee, did you?"

"No."

"Do you know why all those lights are on in Kentucky?"

"No."

"They're watching the replay of our game tonight," Coach Hall said. "Those fans are staying up, and everybody's at home. They've got the TV on, and they're watching the replay of our game against Georgia."

"Come on, Coach!" I thought he was joking.

"That is a fact," he said. "You know you're in Kentucky on a Monday night after a game because those TV sets are on. They aren't on in Tennessee, but they are on here in Kentucky."

Another lesson came during my freshman year when I was dribbling the ball as the UK band played "My Old Kentucky Home" during a pregame warm-up, which was a no-no. Coach Hall came up to me and said, "I know you're from Ohio, but do we have to give you a history lesson about the state of Kentucky? When 'My Old Kentucky Home' is played, it's like the national anthem. This is a very important time of your life. For this one and a half minutes you're going to stand straight up, sing the song, and learn the words."

I played at UK during the head coach transition from Adolph Rupp to Joe B. Hall. One of the holdovers from the Rupp years was Dr. V. A. Jackson, who was our team physician. He traveled with us, was at every practice, and he became a strong support for me. He believed in me more than I believed in myself. He would come up to me and say, "Kevin, I've seen a lot of players come through here: Larry Steele, Mike Pratt, and Pat Riley, and you're as good as any one of those guys."

Sometimes you get beaten down by your coaches and your teammates—you're fighting and battling and trying to get better. When we would have a bad night or a bad game, Dr. Jackson was always a voice of reason and support. He was knowledgeable not just about the history of UK basketball but about the history of the Commonwealth of Kentucky. Listening to him was like listening to

Paul Harvey tell a story. He and his wife would sometimes invite me to their home for a home-cooked meal, which was always special.

The first car I ever bought was Dr. Jackson's black 1973 El Dorado Cadillac with white leather interior. When I signed my NBA contract with the Washington Bullets and got my bonus, I said to him, "Dr. Jackson, I'm going to Washington. I sure love that car."

"Well, do you want to buy it?"

"Are you kidding me?" I replied. "I would love that car."

"I'll get you a price for it," he said. "I'll get it all cleaned up, and you can drive it to Washington."

And I did. I had that car my rookie year in Washington.

Another influential person with Kentucky ties is my long-time friend Jim Duff.[1] Jim and I grew up together in Hamilton and attended the same junior high and high school. His parents were Kentucky natives, and his grandparents had a farm near Cynthiana, where he would spend almost every summer.

Jim and I were teammates on my high school basketball team. He didn't get much playing time, but he once asked me, "Why isn't the University of Kentucky recruiting you? Would you mind if I had my father call Coach Hall?"

Before I knew it, Jim's father, Cecil, made contact with Coach Hall on my behalf. Coach Hall told him, "Yeah, we'll come up to Hamilton. We've heard of this kid." That started my recruiting process.

Jim got accepted at UK about the same time I signed to play there. I asked Coach Hall if he could try out for the freshman basketball team. "You tell Jim Duff that if he tries out for the team, he's on it," Coach Hall said. Our freshman team that year had a record of 22–0. Jim was my link to UK and my grounding force. To me, he was a voice of intelligence and reason. He was such a good guy to have on the team and to this day is one of my best friends.

I return to Lexington occasionally for games, events, and

alumni functions, and UK fans just don't forget you. Once you've worn that uniform, you're in a special fraternity. They're very knowledgeable, passionate fans. During the college basketball season I travel around the country doing color commentary for Westwood One Dial Global Sports. I've worked the NCAA Tournament and conference tournaments and have been to most of the Division I arenas in the United States, and there's no place like UK. No school has the combination of a great facility, passionate fans, rich tradition, beautiful state, a fabulous school. It's got it all.

14

Jack ("Goose") Givens

Named Kentucky's "Mr. Basketball" in 1974 as a senior at Bryan Station High School in Lexington, Jack ("Goose") Givens played four years at UK and scored 2,038 points, which ranks him third on the program's list of all-time leading scorers. He scored 41 points in UK's 94–88 win over Duke University in the 1978 NCAA Men's Basketball Championship game and was named the Final Four Most Outstanding Player that year.

After a two-year career playing for the NBA's Atlanta Hawks, Givens became an NBA color analyst, including stints with Turner Broadcasting System and the Orlando Magic. In 2004 he became president and CEO of the Orlando Comets, a basketball organization sponsored by Nike that helps young female players prepare for the opportunity to compete for full NCAA basketball scholarships.

In the summer of 2012, Givens relocated to Union, Kentucky, where he serves as vice president of business development and external affairs for the Bowlin Group LLC. He and his wife, Linda, have two children: Jeremy and Jaimie.

Jack Givens cuts down the net after the 1978 NCAA Championship game between UK and Duke. (Courtesy of the *Lexington Herald-Leader*. Photo by Frank Anderson.)

I grew up in Lexington, so many of the people who impacted me or played a big role during my time as a player for UK were the same people I had been around all my life: my family, my friends from Bryan Station High School, and members of Greater Liberty Baptist Church, which was my home church. I was fortunate to be able to stay at home and attend UK. That provided me with certain luxuries that a lot of players don't have. I didn't have to leave my hometown and form a lot of new relationships, and when I needed a meal I could go home and enjoy a hot meal. If I needed my clothes washed, I could always go to my mom and she would do my laundry.

Greater Liberty Baptist Church was led by Rev. Albert B. Lee, who was the father of my teammate James Lee. Reverend Lee was influential to me. As is the case in a lot of communities—particularly in inner-city areas—the pastor serves a lot of different roles, not just as the church leader. To a lot of us young congregation members who didn't have a father figure in the home Reverend Lee was a father figure as well. He always gave good advice, and he would compliment me just as he would his son, James. He would also be stern with me, just as he would be with James. I remember him as an encourager and a motivator. He always had a positive word to say when he saw me in church on Sundays.

It seemed like everyone at Greater Liberty Baptist Church was interested in how things were going for me and James and how we were playing. I think Reverend Lee made sure that everyone in our church was doing some extra praying for us, to pray that we stay healthy and that we would continue to be productive.

There were times when James and Coach Joe B. Hall would not see eye-to-eye. In fact, there were times when James was ready to quit the team and head home. When that would happen Reverend Lee asked me to help him convince James that everything would be okay. One time James was upset that Coach Hall had asked him to do some extra running. Reverend Lee asked me why this was the case. I told him it was because James didn't finish the run in the time he was supposed to complete it in. When Reverend Lee heard this he went back to James and told him, "If you're not doing what you're supposed to be doing, it's your fault, not the coach's fault." Reverend Lee was fair, but he was a disciplinarian. He wouldn't hold anything back. If you went to his church it was like you were one of his kids. He would treat us like he would treat James.

Another person influential to me was Bill Keightley, the long-time equipment manager for the men's basketball program. He was always one to give advice and a shoulder to cry on when I had a bad game, when practices were hard, or when coaches would be on my case. He always had a positive word to say. He would share stories of tough times some of the players who preceded me went through, including those who played for Coach Adolph Rupp. Even after my career at UK—anytime I came back to Lexington to watch a practice or a game—he still had stories to tell. I know that he shared stories about some of my struggles with players who succeeded me.

Bill was with us at every practice, every game, every meal, and he knew all of us players well. He was very good at picking up on our personalities, and he had a way of making you feel like you were the most important player on the team. Bill also understood that Coach Hall's nature was to get on the captain of the team more than everyone else. His philosophy was that everyone would know that if he got on the captain of the team for not doing what he thought he should be doing, then that was open season for him to get on everyone. I was a team captain three out of my four years at UK, so Coach Hall would get on my case when he was trying to send a message to everyone on the team. When that happened and I'd get frustrated, Bill's main advice to me was to let it go in one ear and come out the other. He would always tell me that.

Bill also talked to the coaches a lot, so he kind of knew what they were thinking and the reasons why they gave us players a hard time now and then. He was creative and discreet in relaying that information to you. He wouldn't come right out and say, "The coaches told me this," but you just kind of knew that they were the source of the information he shared with you.

To this day the most influential person in my life has been my mother, Betty. I grew up in a housing project on the east side of Lexington. I was one of ten kids, and we didn't have some of the other "stuff" that a lot of kids in our neighborhood had. That's not to say that other kids I grew up with had a lot either, but for me and my nine siblings there was just not a lot of room for extra "stuff." The thing that I appreciate most about my mom is that she never allowed us to dwell on the things we didn't have, but be grateful for what we did have. There was never a time I can remember when we didn't have food to eat, although at times I would have liked more. We always had clean clothes to wear, even though they might have been hand-me-downs from my older brothers. Mom went to work every day, and at times she had two jobs to make sure we had the things we needed. Another amazing thing about my mom is that she never refused to take in other kids, cousins and anyone else from the neighborhood who needed a meal or a place to hang out. I know all of the lessons I learned from Mom have helped mold me into the person I am today.

UK fans also played a part in my success. There are no better college basketball fans in the country than UK fans. They follow basketball every day every year, not just during the basketball season. They're well aware of what's going on with the program and follow the top recruits from the time those players are in high school.

The atmosphere around today's UK players is different than it was in my era because back then most basketball players stayed in college for four years. This enabled fans to get to know the players a whole lot better than they do today. Of course, fans want these great players to stay in school as long as they can to win games for the program, but I think the real issue is that UK fans pride themselves on getting to know the players personally and intimately. That's harder to do in today's "one and done" climate, with some players staying in college just one or two years before moving on to careers in the NBA.

Even in the current "one and done" environment, though, UK fans follow the teams with a level of interest that you don't see with other programs. After my career at UK I played for the NBA's Atlanta Hawks. Regardless of what city the Hawks were playing in—be it Atlanta, Seattle, Los Angeles, Denver, or Cleveland—there would always be Kentucky fans in the stands wearing UK t-shirts and caps, showing support for me. They'd bring me cookies or items to be autographed. My teammates and other NBA players were surprised by the coast-to-coast support I received from Kentucky fans.

When I was being recruited by UK, fans would pack the gym at Bryan Station High School to watch me play. Many of those crowds were standing-room only. I'd hear things from fans like, "You'd look good in Kentucky blue." The support those fans offered was amazing.

Even today, when I travel in the Commonwealth people still recognize me and sometimes treat me like I played in Rupp Arena last year. It's surprising to me how many people are well versed in my career—even people of high school age—and how many doors my career at UK opened for me from a business standpoint. It has allowed me access to people that otherwise I may not have been able to get to. Fans just don't forget former players, and it helps you in everything you do.

To this day fans send *Sports Illustrated* covers[1] from 1978 and other items for me to autograph. That's part of Kentucky basketball.

15

Rick Robey

Center Rick Robey tallied 1,395 points during his four-year career, ranking him twenty-third on the list of all-time leading scorers in the program's history. As a freshman he led the Wildcats in field-goal percentage (.544) and in free-throw percentage (.810), and he pulled down a total of 838 rebounds during his career, which ranks him ninth in that category among all former UK players. As a junior and senior he led the team in rebounding, averaging 9.1 and 8.2 rebounds per game, respectively.

Robey scored twenty points and grabbed eleven rebounds in UK's 94–88 victory over Duke University on March 27, 1978. Later that year he was the third overall pick in the NBA draft, selected by the Indiana Pacers. He played a total of eight seasons in the NBA, including stints with the Boston Celtics, where he was a member of that team's 1981 NBA Championship squad, and the Phoenix Suns.

In the early 1990s Robey and his wife, Bonnie, moved to Louisville, where the couple began careers in the real estate industry. Today he is a realtor with the Robey and Farrar RE/MAX team in Louisville, and Bonnie is a mortgage broker. Their son, Sam, played varsity football for the University of Florida and graduated from the university in 2013.

Rick Robey credits Adolph Rupp with facilitating a chance for him to try out for a spot on the US team that competed in the 1975 Pan American Games. He made the squad, and the team won the gold medal. (Courtesy of the University of Kentucky Archives.)

One native Kentuckian who influenced me was my UK coach, Joe B. Hall. Coach Hall was a real disciplinarian who shot from the hip. Not all players liked his style, but I think when they got a little bit older they realized Coach Hall was on them because he wanted to make them better as players and as people. That's one thing I learned early on: if Joe B. wasn't chewing my ass out, he no longer thought I could get any better as a player, so I was hoping every day he was chewing on me, because he was just trying to make me a better player and a better person.

When I first arrived on campus Coach Hall said, "Rick, if you do what I tell you to do, you will become as good a player as you ever want to be." I sure didn't believe that at the time, but I ended up being the number-three pick in the 1978 NBA draft. I achieved that, I think, because of what Coach Hall instilled in me as far as taking off-season workouts seriously and doing what I needed to do to become a better player.

Seth W. Hancock is another native Kentuckian who played a huge role in my life during my playing days at UK. After Seth's father, Arthur B. Hancock, passed away in 1972, Seth took over the family business, operating Claiborne Farm near Paris, Kentucky, which is probably the most world-renowned breeding farm for Thoroughbred horses. Seth hired me to work at the farm during the summers, and he was only about four years older than me. I had an interest in horses at the time, and I still do. I'd muck stalls, bring in the yearlings, and groom the horses. In fact, the great black filly Ruffian was a yearling in one of the fields I took care of.

Some people thought I was working at Claiborne Farm for favors, but Seth wasn't that type of person. If I was late for work, I got docked. If I didn't show up for work, I got docked, and I got penalized. He made me accountable. He was one of those pointed types of people who made me a better person not only off the basketball court but on the basketball court as well. I wouldn't say we were great friends right at the beginning of my working at Claiborne, but the older we became, we developed a great friendship. In fact, his son, Walker, enrolled at the University of Florida about the same time my son, Sam, went there to play football, so our friendship was rekindled again, with our boys going off to the same university. What's more, on June 7, 2012, Seth and I were inducted into the Kentucky Athletic Hall of Fame. That was a memorable night.

My father, Fred, always played a huge role in everything I did. He wasn't from Kentucky, but he never missed one of my college games. He was in charge of the southeastern region for his business, so he had a lot of offices in the proximity of Southeastern Conference schools and was able to come to all of my games.

My father was always there for me. That's what I try to do for my son, Sam. I attended every University of Florida Gators football game to cheer him on, no matter what.

Another person who was very dear to me was Bill Keightley. We were big lunch buddies. Since he worked the mail route around campus we would meet up for lunch quite often. He was kind of a father figure to me, and if you were ever having a bad day he could always pick you up. He always called me Bear.

I didn't realize until later in life what an important part Coach Adolph Rupp played in my career. He was retired from UK at the time, but he was instrumental in helping me get invited to tryouts to represent the United States in the 1975 Pan American Games. Freshmen weren't invited at the time, but Coach Rupp had some pull, so I was among the 170 to 180 players invited to try out. I ultimately made the twelve-man roster for the US team, and that certainly was a big boost to my career. Our team won the gold medal in those games, and my teammates included Otis Birdsong, Johnny Davis, and Robert Parish, who became my teammate again when I joined the Boston Celtics during my NBA career.

After my UK career people would come up to me and show a

picture of me standing with them when I was a UK player. They'd
say, "Remember this day?" If I had known as a player the magnitude
of the support I'd receive from fans and what UK basketball meant
to so many people, I might not have been able to play, because my
nerves might not have been able to handle it. Kentucky fans are second to none. They supported me when I played in the NBA and was
matched up against former Kentucky players. Dan Issel and I played
against each other. I'd go out onto the floor and say, "Dan, remember I'm a former Kentucky player. Don't hurt me too bad tonight."

I remember the first time I flew into Lexington as a recruit in
1974. When we landed the first thing I saw was a white house with
a sign that read "Welcome to Wildcat Country." I was from New
Orleans, which is a big city, and I didn't understand how big the tradition of UK basketball was. I remember talking to my dad on the
phone that night and saying, "Where in the heck did you send me?"
But what I've come to learn and appreciate from 1974 to this day is
that you won't find a better fan base or people that love their basketball like UK fans. Today I spoke at two basketball camps for young
kids, because I'm an old Kentucky player. Every day somebody asks
me something about Kentucky basketball. That's what makes it very
special.

I chose to settle in Kentucky after my pro career. It's where
I wanted to raise my family. People are so friendly here. Being a
former athlete from UK opens doors for you in the business community, but you still have to do your job. If you do your job, good
things could happen for you.

16

Kyle Macy

Named Indiana's "Mr. Basketball" in 1975 as a high school senior, guard Kyle Macy transferred to UK after playing his freshman year at Purdue University. He tallied 1,411 points during his three seasons at UK, which ranks him twenty-first on the list of the program's all-time leading scorers.

Macy led UK in assists and in free-throw percentage during each of his three years and finished his career with a total of 470 assists (sixth all-time) and a free-throw percentage of 89 percent (tied with Jodie Meeks for all-time leader in the category, with a minimum of two hundred free-throw attempts). He also led the Wildcats in steals during the 1978–1979 and 1979–1980 campaigns (sixty-nine and fifty-eight steals, respectively).

A two-time All-American, Macy was the floor general during UK's 94–88 victory over Duke University in the 1978 NCAA National Championship game. He scored nine points and dished out eight assists in that contest.

Macy spent seven years in the NBA, playing for the Phoenix Suns, Chicago Bulls, and Indiana Pacers. He coached the Morehead State University Eagles from 1997 to 2006 and was inducted into the Indi-

A two-time All-American, Kyle Macy was named SEC Player of the Year in 1980. (Courtesy of the University of Kentucky Archives.)

ana Basketball Hall of Fame in 2001. He currently teaches tennis in the Lexington area and is a color commentator for UK basketball telecasts. He and his wife, Tina, have two daughters, Mallory and Meredith, and a son, Malone. The family lives in Lexington.

I consider myself a Kentuckian because I've lived here longer than anyplace else during my life, but I grew up in Peru, Indiana. My father, Bob Macy, taught me how to play basketball and taught me all the basic fundamentals of the game. He was a fine player and coach in his own right, and he was inducted into the Indiana Basketball Hall of Fame in 1996. In fact, he coached me at Peru High School, where I played. My mom was another important influence on me. Since my dad was my high school coach, the old phrase "leave it on the court" didn't apply to us. During meals at home my mom would often play referee with me and my dad over discussions we had about a practice or a game. She was a calming influence. They both had an impact on me: Dad a lot more about life on the court and Mom a lot more about life off the court.

When I arrived at UK as a transfer from Purdue University, Coach Joe B. Hall became an important influence. To me he instilled a sense of discipline and the importance of working hard, whether during the regular season or during the off-season. He also stressed the importance of keeping in shape by hitting the weight room and running sprints. Sometimes he would yell at me and other players to get us motivated. In the locker room prior to our matchup with Tennessee during my senior year, Coach Hall started saying that I wanted to do more on the floor to help the team. It was almost like he was trying to embarrass me in front of my teammates, saying things like, "Macy, you talk about wanting to do this and that. Tonight you're going to get your chance. We're going to play a two-man game on top with you and [Sam] Bowie in the pick and roll."

He was challenging me. It worked, because I was fired up. I had over twenty points in that game, I think, and we won. That's one way to get a player motivated.

Before we played in the Final Four in St. Louis in 1978 we had a team gathering after our mandatory shoot-around, without the coaches. A couple of the seniors on our team said, "Look. Our goal wasn't just to get here, so let's relax and keep focused on what we're trying to do, and that's win the national championship." That illustrates how self-motivated that entire team was. We were listening to our coaches, of course, but we were focused. We knew the task at hand and how we were going to accomplish it. What carried us to victory in the 1978 NCAA Championship game, I think, was that each of us players motivated ourselves as well as our teammates. If somebody would have an off day in practice we'd say things to that teammate like, "Come on, pick it up. You can do better." We encouraged each other. There were a lot of times when I did not feel like running twelve, fifteen, or seventeen 220-yard sprints in thirty-two seconds back to back—which was part of our conditioning program. But the mental toughness you develop and the discipline to fight through and do the dirty work only benefits you.

Those lessons followed me to my career in the NBA and in my later coaching career at Morehead State University, especially the discipline components, emphasizing the importance of doing what you're supposed to do, when you're supposed to do it, and doing it to the best of your ability each and every time. If you can bring that sense of focus to any aspect of your life, good things are going to happen. There were times when I was coaching at Morehead State when I'd hear myself say something to the team and I'd think to myself, "That sounds like Coach Hall!"

Assistant Coach Dick Parsons also had an influence on me. He was a counterbalance to Coach Hall, who would often get fired up about things. Coach Parsons would too, but in a different way, in a more quiet way. He always got his point across though. Even during the course of a game, if Coach Hall was going off on the officials, Coach Parsons had a way of getting Coach Hall's attention back on the game and on the players. He would encourage us, and he wouldn't let us get down.

Coach Parsons played at UK when he was a student, so that gave him credibility with the players. He spent a lot of time with the team because he was in charge of our fall conditioning program. For that program we would dress at Memorial Coliseum and jog over to the track. Coach Parsons would jog over there and back with us and would often lead the way. He wouldn't do the sprints with us, but he was very fit. From a motivational standpoint he was positive. He got some players to break through barriers where they'd run a 220-yard sprint, for example, and didn't feel like they could do any more.

We were at the track every Monday, Wednesday, and Friday. On Tuesdays and Thursdays we'd play pickup games. At the track we would run anywhere from three to seventeen 220-yard sprints. We'd run a 220-yard sprint and walk back to the starting line. We had to make that distance in thirty-two seconds, with about a one-and-a-half-minute rest before running the next sprint. We were in good shape. From there we'd go to the weight room for about one and a half hours and then jog back to Memorial Coliseum.

Another Kentuckian who was special to me during my days as a player was Katharine Hall, Coach Hall's wife. The year I sat out as a transfer student I got sicker than a dog right before the basketball team left town for a road trip during the winter break. I think it was from food poisoning. The dorms were empty, so the Halls invited me to stay at their house. Katharine took care of me there for a day or two until I got better, and she made sure that I was eating well. That made a big impression on me. Here I was, a new transfer student, and she was caring enough to look after me like that. If anyone on the team had a problem Katharine was more than willing to help, whether it meant bringing soup over when we were sick or just keeping an eye on us. She was like a team mother. At least once a year the Halls would have the whole team out to their house for a meal.

Bill Keightley was also influential. The year I sat out as a transfer student I was not allowed to travel with the team. At that time Bill wasn't traveling much with the team. During those times he'd open up the gym for me and get me a ball so I could work out, but afterward he always took time to talk with me. He'd encourage me, not only in basketball but in life in general. He was a friend.

Bob Bradley,[1] who was in charge of UK's academic center for student-athletes, impacted me in a remote way. When I arrived on campus he explained that players who didn't maintain a certain grade point average would have to attend a mandatory study hall every evening. That motivated me to keep my GPA above that cutoff so I wouldn't have to attend those mandatory study halls. Thankfully I achieved that goal. I wanted to have a semblance of a normal life as a college student, not just basketball, study hall, and right back to the school the next morning. I'm still good friends with Bob.

The loyalty of Big Blue Nation is hard to explain. You almost have to live through it to get a feel for how loyal and sincere fans are and how people love basketball in Kentucky. One year our team traveled to Freedom Hall in Louisville to play a New Year's Eve game against Notre Dame. We had an open practice the morning of the game, and fans packed the arena. It was a chance for people who didn't have season tickets to watch about an hour of our practice, and then we signed autographs for about thirty minutes afterward. Tables were set up all around the court for the autograph session. I was tabled next to Rick Robey. There was such a big push by the crowd that one of the tables collapsed. Then, all of a sudden I heard a commotion from Rick's table. Someone had come up behind him and tried to clip a lock of his hair with scissors!

Of course, UK basketball fans had an impact on me, and they

still do. When I was playing in the NBA, competing in arenas in every corner of the United States, it seemed like there was always a Kentucky fan who'd yell, "Hey, Macy!" during pre-game warm-ups or recollect some memory they had about the Kentucky program. That made me feel at home no matter where I was. It gave me a lot of confidence as a player knowing that I played against the best and with the best. Now, as a member of the Lexington community, the relationship with fans persists. They're more than kind in sharing stories of my playing days from a long time ago. It's a nice feeling.

17

Derrick Hord

A native of Bristol, Tennessee, guard/forward Derrick Hord was a Parade *All-American and a McDonald's All-American at Tennessee High School. During his four years at UK, Hord scored 1,220 points, ranking him thirty-eighth on the list of the program's all-time leading scorers. He led the 1981–1982 squad in scoring, averaging 16.3 points per game, and he led the 1982–1983 squad in free-throw percentage (.823).*

After his UK career he was drafted by the Cleveland Cavaliers in the third round of the 1983 NBA draft before going on to play one year of professional basketball in Japan.

Today Hord is a physician recruiter for Baptist Health Lexington. He also serves on the board of directors for the Kentucky State Parks Association. He and his wife, Lisa, live in Lexington with their daughter, Kaitlyn.

Derrick Hord earned All-SEC honors in 1982 and finished his career with a field-goal percentage of 47 percent. (Courtesy of *The Cats' Pause*.)

I grew up in Bristol, Tennessee, which is just over an hour from the campus of the University of Tennessee. Back then the basketball rivalry between the Wildcats and the Volunteers was intense, but my personal introduction to the UK program came about because of Larry Qualls, a Bristol resident who had relatives that lived in Kentucky. Larry's sons, Kent and Kevin, were close to me in age, and we became good friends. The Qualls were pro-ability water-skiers, and they used to take me out waterskiing in the summers. In fact, they taught me how to waterski. Kent and Kevin always seemed to be wearing shorts or t-shirts with the word "Kentucky" or the UK Wildcat logo printed on them. That intrigued me.

During basketball season my sophomore year of high school I remember being a guest at the Qualls' house for dinner. Their house was located in the hills of Bristol, and I noticed Larry pacing around in the back yard. After a while I asked Kent and Kevin, "What's your dad doing?" It turns out he was listening to Cawood Ledford call a Kentucky basketball game on a small transistor radio. They explained that he couldn't get the broadcast signal on their good family radio, but Larry could pick it up on the transistor radio. I was amazed. Here was this avid UK fan in Bristol going to great lengths to keep up with the team. That piqued my curiosity.

The school I had long dreamed of playing basketball for was the University of Notre Dame, and the Qualls knew that. In 1977 they bought tickets to UK's annual matchup with Notre Dame at Freedom Hall in Louisville, and they included me. We drove up to the game in a motor home, and I was the sole Notre Dame fan on board. But by the time the game was over I was a UK fan. I was blown away by the fans who turned out at Freedom Hall and by the way Kentucky played—just the overall atmosphere. I remember saying to myself, "Wow. This is something." At that moment I put UK on the radar, and my interest grew from there. I attended basketball camps at UK, talked to the coaches, and they won me over.

When it became evident that I was starting to favor UK, Marshall Harris, my best friend since kindergarten, started liking the idea as well. He was the head manager of our high school basketball team, and we'd watch a lot of UK games together. Eventually, when I decided to attend UK, Marshall was offered an academic scholarship there. So we left Bristol for Lexington together, and he became a manager for the UK basketball team.

When I arrived at UK I was offered a summer job working for a small company owned by the late Dick Broadbent. He was a visionary who started a computer service that statistically computed what kind of foal an X mare and a Y stallion would produce. The Jockey Club and other organizations provide that service now, but at the time Mr. Broadbent's service was in high demand. Even though it was a small corporation I learned a little bit about corporate life from him. To me Mr. Broadbent was like a coach outside of basketball. He was tough. He was gruff. He demanded the most out of his employees. In some respects it coincided with the way UK basketball was: give your all while you're there, be accountable—that kind of thing. I appreciated the opportunity to learn something like that so early in my college education.

Marta McMackin, UK basketball's longtime secretary, was the glue that held a lot of things together for coaches, players, and fans. She was like family, and that's what she became. She was a bridge to the coaches. If I'd call over to the basketball office she was the first person who would pick up the phone for whatever coach I was trying to reach. She was very helpful, and to this day we exchange Christmas cards and are very close. In my opinion it's unfortunate that people like her are not still involved with the program in some capacity, especially since the passing of Bill Keightley. She is one of the last links that bridge the past era of UK basketball to the present.

Glenn and Marian Sims of Lexington also became like family to me. Glenn had been a manager on Coach Rupp's staff. When

I first arrived at UK they gave me keys to their house and invited me to go there to get away from university life. If I wanted to have a home-cooked meal they were always there for me. Glenn passed away in the early 2000s, but I still keep in contact with Marian and their son, Andy, who was like a little brother to me. In fact, when I was playing for UK the movie *Rocky,* starring Sylvester Stallone, was popular. Andy named his cat "Rocky Balboa Hord." It seemed like that cat lived for a long, long time. To this day when I see Andy we laugh about that.

The late George Middleton, an avid golfer who worked at the University of Kentucky, was another important person to me. He and his wife befriended players like me and invited us over to their house for dinner. In fact, they hosted me for my first Thanksgiving dinner away from home. They were always supportive.

I'd be remiss if I didn't mention the late Louis Stout, who was the commissioner of the Kentucky High School Athletic Association from 1994 to 2002. He was the first African American in the nation to lead a state athletic association. Louis later became president of the national Amateur Athletic Union (AAU) before he died in 2012. Louis was from Coach Joe B. Hall's hometown of Cynthiana, Kentucky, and he played basketball at Regis College in Denver, Colorado, during Coach Hall's tenure there. Had the times been different he could have become the first African American player at UK. When I arrived at UK Louis provided insight to me on many areas, including UK basketball, Coach Hall, and life in general. He served on all kinds of boards in the community and was a positive influence. He was just a dynamite guy.

The loyal UK fan base had a huge impact on why I chose to become a Wildcat. Wherever you go in this state people identify with the basketball program. It's like they all take ownership of it; it's theirs. At my high school in Tennessee the student body supported our basketball team with passion. I noticed an immediate similarity when I came to see a UK game; it helped me make the transition from high school to college much easier. There's no other program like it. I'm thankful and I'm grateful that I had the opportunity to play there.

Part III

The 1980s–1990s

In the first matchup between the Louisville Cardinals and the Kentucky Wildcats since 1959, the Cards defeated UK 80–68 on March 26, 1983, to earn a spot in that year's Final Four. Two years later, Joe B. Hall retired after thirteen seasons as head coach, ending his career with an overall record of 297–100 (75 percent). UK hired former Creighton University and University of Arkansas coach Eddie Sutton to succeed Hall.

In Sutton's first season as head coach the Wildcats finished with a 32–4 record. Junior Kenny "Sky" Walker led the Wildcats in scoring that year, averaging 22.9 points per contest. Walker went on to score 2,080 points during his career, second only to Dan Issel. Another standout player, Owensboro, Kentucky, native Rex Chapman, arrived on the scene for the 1986–1987 campaign. An exceptional leaper, Chapman led the Wildcats in scoring during his freshman and sophomore years, averaging 16 and 19 points per game, respectively.

The 1980s ended on a sour note. Not only did the Wildcats close out the 1988–1989 season with their first losing record in sixty-one seasons, but the NCAA launched an investigation into UK recruiting and academic violations. The scandal led to Sutton's resignation on March 19, 1989. Two months later, the NCAA placed the storied program on three years' probation, including a ban from postseason competition in 1990 and 1991. On June 2, 1989, former Boston University and Providence College coach Rick Pitino was named UK's new basketball coach.

After his first season Pitino landed heralded recruit Jamal Mashburn, a player whom many experts credit with leading the way for other blue-chip players to follow after UK's NCAA probation. During his sophomore year, Mashburn led UK in scoring, averaging twenty-one points per game as a member of "The Unforgettables." That team was inched out of a trip to the Final Four after Duke University's Christian Laettner hit a last-second shot in overtime during the East Regional finals on March 28, 1992. Four years later Pitino led UK to its sixth national title, a 76–67 win over Syracuse University on April 1, 1996.

UK earned an opportunity to defend its national title on March 31, 1997, but fell to the Arizona Wildcats 84–79. Six weeks later Pitino resigned, accepting an offer to become president and head coach of the Boston Celtics. He finished his career at UK with a 219–50 record (81 percent). Orlando ("Tubby") Smith, who had served as Pitino's assistant coach for two years, was named the program's new head coach. In his first year Smith led the Wildcats to a 35–4 record, which culminated in UK's seventh national title, a 78–69 victory over Utah on March 30, 1998.

18

Jim Master

Named Indiana's "Mr. Basketball" in 1980 as a high school senior and a McDonald's All-American the same year, guard Jim Master was part of a UK freshman class that included Bret Bearup, Dicky Beal, and the late Melvin Turpin.

During his four years as a Wildcat, Master scored 1,283 points, ranking him thirty-first on the list of the program's all-time leading scorers. He ranks fourth all-time in free-throw percentage among UK players who attempted a minimum of two hundred free throws during their career (.849). As a sophomore he led the 1981–1982 squad in free-throw percentage (.896) and made forty consecutive free throws that season, ranking him second in that category behind Travis Ford.

Following his junior year Master was a member of the US gold medal team at the 1983 Pan American Games in Caracas, Venezuela. That team featured several future NBA stars, including Michael Jordan, Chris Mullin, Sam Perkins, and Mark Price.

Today Master is a financial advisor at Hilliard Lyons in Lexington, where he works with his brother, Randal. He and his wife, Sheila, live in Lexington with their son, Leo.

Jim Master (20) contests a shot during a matchup against the University of Illinois in Rupp Arena. Also pictured, left to right, are teammates Sam Bowie and Kenny ("Sky") Walker. (Courtesy of the University of Kentucky Archives.)

The first time I ever visited Lexington I met Donald[1] and Dudley Webb. The Webb brothers were shakers and movers back in that time, constructing buildings all over the country. I remember sitting with them in Rupp Arena when I came here on an official visit to watch a UK basketball game, and we remained friends. Just being able to associate with them as a student was special. In the summers they'd invite me to swim in their swimming pool.

During my freshman year I met the late coal baron Thomas "Brown" Badgett Sr. He supported the university with his money, his backing, and his time. I considered him the Ernest Hemingway of his time because of his strong interest in fishing. After I graduated from UK he and I became such good friends that I went on several fishing trips with him throughout the world on his private jet, which had room for two pilots and eight passengers. Joe B. Hall would often go with us, and C. M. Newton—who likes to bonefish—went on some trips with us as well. My favorite trips were the ones to Venezuela. We must have flown there seven times in a period of three years. We'd fly into Caracas and then get on propeller planes that flew us to a private camp in the middle of the jungle where we spent almost one week fishing for peacock bass. Brown Badgett was an amazing, smart human being who was a big influence on me the last twenty-five years of his life.

I also became close to the late James Lawrence ("Jim") Rose, who was a coal baron from London, Kentucky, and a big friend of the UK basketball program. I got to know his wife, Judy, and their family extremely well. In fact, my parents would stay at their home in London when they traveled from Indiana to watch the Wildcats play at the University of Tennessee in Knoxville and at other SEC schools in the South, as a way to break up the trip.

Seth Hancock, the owner of Claiborne Farm, was another big influence on me during my early days at UK. I had a summer job working on one of his horse farms when I was a student, and I still see Seth now and then. I think the world of his knowledge and of his success. He has a lot of good traits—including honesty and respect—and he taught me how to conduct myself in a good way. Of course, his business knowledge is very good, and his horse knowledge is probably second to none. I met a lot of interesting and important people through him, whether we were at the Kentucky Derby or just driving around town.

I think I played in the greatest state for high school basketball back in Indiana, and I played in the greatest place to play college basketball at UK. The reason is the fan base. It was difficult for me to comprehend at first how much people get into basketball here. Rupp Arena would be packed for a scrimmage. Back then we'd play four practice scrimmages in smaller towns across the state before we'd start our season. The enthusiasm for those games was amazing. We'd go to places like Hazard, and the whole town would shut down. Fans would put up signs with messages like, "Here come the 'Cats!"

At the end of the basketball season there would be two to three hundred requests for UK players to appear at events throughout the state, maybe be the guest speaker at a high school freshman banquet or be the parade marshal at the annual Hazard Christmas Parade. Our basketball office would be inundated with these requests every year. Some of us liked to do those things because we got to meet some important, influential people all over the state. I did a few of them and met some great people, some shakers and movers in the community.

The support for UK basketball was unreal to me as a player, and I continue to be reminded how strong the following is, even though I played my last game as a Wildcat in 1984. I still get twenty or thirty fan letters each year. Almost all of them deal with requests for autographs. They'll send a picture of me when I played, or they'll send cards that people made of me back then. Another reminder of the widespread popularity of UK basketball came to me in December 2012 when I attended an NCAA Football Hall of Fame induction luncheon at the 21 Club in New York City. I was seated at a table with former University of Tennessee football halfback Johnny Majors, who was a runner-up for the Heisman Trophy in 1956 and who coached the University of Pittsburgh Panthers to an NCAA National Championship in 1976. I was in awe to meet him, but all he wanted to talk about was UK basketball! He said, "Jim, in Tennessee I grew up listening to Cawood Ledford call those UK games." A similar thing happened when I met the former Chicago Bears great Mike Ditka for the first time playing a round of golf. I wanted to talk to him about his great career as a player and coach, but all he wanted to talk about was Kentucky basketball.

What sets UK fans apart from fans of other programs is the deep tradition. Coach Adolph Rupp coached UK to four NCAA National Championships, and the games were broadcast on the radio throughout the state by some legendary people like Cawood Ledford. From then on I think support for the program just spread like wildfire all through the state. Today, the biggest UK Alumni Association chapter is based in Louisville. That's funny to me.

I think my time at UK prepared me to handle some of the ups and downs in life as a human being—from my educational experience as a college student to some of the tough times playing for UK. I realized the value of hard work, earning my degree in four years while having to practice with my teammates six days a week, lift weights, run, and compete in the national spotlight. Couple that with people I met along the way and achieving notoriety—and learning to handle that notoriety—and it's been positive for me. It was special stuff.

19

Roger Harden

Valparaiso, Indiana, native Roger Harden was named the state's "Mr. Basketball" in 1982, his senior season. The guard also earned national recognition as a Parade *and McDonald's All-American, and he finished his career at Valparaiso High School with 1,590 points, which remains a school record.*

At UK, Harden dished out 498 assists during his career, or an average of 4.1 per game, which ranks him third among career leaders in that category. During the 1985–1986 season he dished out 232 assists, or an average of 6.44 per game, which ranks second behind John Wall among single-season leaders in that category. He finished his career with 478 points and a free-throw average of 79 percent.

After UK, Harden was drafted by the Los Angeles Lakers in the 1986 NBA draft. In 2012 he was named the boys' basketball coach at Williamstown (Kentucky) Junior/Senior High School. He lives in Williamstown with his wife, Gina. They have four children: a son, Joseph, and daughters Allison, Sarah, and Olivia.

Roger Harden dished out 232 assists during UK's 1985–1986 campaign, an all-time single-season record that he held for twenty-four years, before John Wall surpassed it in 2010. (Courtesy of *The Cats' Pause*.)

One of the main reasons I signed with UK had to do with the quality of people that Coach Joe B. Hall had around the program. They not only cared about you as a basketball player, but they were very interested in trying to use UK basketball as a positive force for the state of Kentucky. That really is what my teammates and I signed up for. When you come to UK, you understand that Kentucky basketball is life to people. I'm a kid from Indiana who grew up knowing and believing that if you went to play for UK it was a level unlike any other as far as fans living and dying with their basketball team. For an athlete, there's nothing more exhilarating and there's nothing that motivates you more than to represent people who really care about you. To this day fans come up to me and tell me how much they appreciated my career and how much they enjoy UK basketball. That just makes my day.

I came to UK not a very good person and left a higher-quality person. Many of us who wore Wildcat uniforms from my era were not only "Mr. Basketball" in our state; we were often among the top players in the country at our position. You can arrive at Kentucky a little delusional from the standpoint of ego, and it can get worse if you believe the hype that's said and written about you. When you're on the inside of the basketball program you have to stay centered. That can be very difficult for young people at first. It's like being part of a boy band. That's the life you're living.

Right before my sophomore year at UK I became a father to my son, Joseph. When I learned I was going to be a father, the first person I turned to was Chuck Melcher,[1] the local Campus Crusade for Christ director at the time. He and his wife, Charlotte, not only had a profound impact on my spirituality, but they were friends at a time when I really needed them. They helped me to accept the responsibility of becoming a father and to understand how this was going to change my life, and how I was going to have to change my whole outlook on life. I had to assure Joseph's mother that I was going to be responsible financially; I was not going to walk away from my responsibility. I give her a lot of credit for bringing Joseph into the world, because she had an opportunity to make other decisions. I can't imagine life without Joseph. Because I embraced the responsibility, he was the best thing that ever happened to me while I was at UK, bar none. He made me a better man.

Back home in Indiana, my parents, Al and Myrna, were supportive of my situation, but they knew I was going to have to grow up quickly. It was more important to my parents that I be the best dad I could be than that I be a collegiate All-American. After Joseph arrived, the first questions they asked when I called home had nothing to do with basketball. They asked questions like, "What's going on with your son? When are you going to see him again? Is there anything we need to do to help you?"

Both Coach Hall and Coach Eddie Sutton had wonderful impacts on me. Coach Hall gave me the opportunity of a lifetime. When he sat across from me at a table, pulled out a letter of intent from the University of Kentucky, turned that letter around and slid it over in front of me and said, "I want you to be our point guard," in my mind, I had arrived from a basketball standpoint. I committed to UK just before my senior year of high school basketball began. I wanted the talk around town to be "How are the Valparaiso Vikings going to do this year?" not "Where's Roger going to college?" We didn't need any distractions.

Coach Hall instilled in us the notion that no one player is bigger than the UK basketball program. He made sure we understood that we represented the greatest franchise in all of college basketball. We felt like representing UK was as big as playing for the Boston Celtics or the Los Angeles Lakers. When the Lakers drafted me it was a big deal, but in my mind playing for UK was bigger.

Because of Coach Sutton's struggles in life, particularly with alcoholism, he always fought his addiction. He knew he had a problem, and he fought it. When he lost the battle he felt bad. From those experiences compassion came out when he coached. When you made a mistake with Coach Sutton, he'd say two positive things about you, and then he'd say, "But until you do A, B, or C, you're never going to be who this team needs you to be." The way he corrected us not only connected with me and changed the way that I played; he also gave me a model of how to treat people in life, such as being willing to help others and to never look down on anyone. When I was a player he frequently checked in on me and wanted to make sure that I was involved in my son's life. Several times I showed up to practice, and I'd tell Coach Sutton I hadn't seen my son in a week. He'd excuse me from practice so I could spend time with my son. And here I was, his starting point guard.

Coach Sutton also taught me to never give up on a player as a coach. I was a student assistant on his staff at UK for two years. When I got behind the scenes and I heard how coaches talk about practice and about the players, I reflected back to my own career and thought, "I wonder what the coaches were saying about me?" In staff meetings with Coach Sutton it became apparent that when you gave advice, he didn't care to hear sentiments such as, "We just need to forget about this kid; he's never going to come around." If you ever said something like that, you got your head handed to you. I've always remembered that. To this day I try to instill in people involved with my basketball program that we never give up on a kid. Once he's made our team we never give up on him, no matter what mistakes he's made. There are a few mistakes that might cost him a college scholarship, but from a basketball standpoint we make a commitment to the kid and do everything we can to help make him better.

If the passion that fans of the Big Blue Nation are famous for were to ever subside, that would be the end of UK basketball; it would become just another program. I understand and appreciate that passion now even more than when I was a player. Every time the Wildcats play—other than on Sunday when I go to church to praise

God—I'm living and dying with the boys. I'm a part of the Big Blue Nation. When the game's over I call five or six people to hash the game out with. When they lose I'm down. It's a way for the people of Kentucky to get away from their lives for a bit. Times are tough right now. We all drop our differences, and we all come together. I love being a part of it.

In my current job as boys' basketball coach at Williamstown (Kentucky) Junior/Senior High School, I'm a little bit of my high school coach mixed with Coach Hall mixed with Coach Sutton and a little dash of Pat Riley. Coaches have different styles, but the most important trait with any coach is that your players have to trust you. They have to trust that you have your best intentions for them. It's possible to play for a coach who's verbally abusive. It's possible to play for a coach who has decided he doesn't like you and he's going to try to run you off the team. But all of my coaches at UK had commitments to me. They weren't going to quit on me. When I came to Kentucky I made a commitment to them, but the commitment they made to me was just as sacred. They took it seriously. They had commitments to their players as people.

I think it's important for young people who play for elite, high-profile college athletic teams to undergo a reality check of sorts, as a way to prevent delusional thinking and disappointment. It's almost as if we need to say something like, "Hey, people are still going to appreciate you after your UK career is over, but if you're not going to continue with athletics beyond college, it's important that you have an outlet after UK. Who's going to be your friend and see you as a human being?" I was fortunate to have good people around me who helped me in the transition after college, but it becomes a struggle for some. You're in the fishbowl one minute, and then, the next thing you know, your career is over, and nobody knows what's going on with you. It's like being the last guy standing in a game of musical chairs. You have to realize that the music's over, and you've got to move on with your life.

20

Deron Feldhaus

Deron Feldhaus was named Kentucky's 1987 Gatorade State Player of the Year at the end of his senior season at Mason County High School in Maysville, where he was coached by his father, former UK player Allen Feldhaus Sr.

Feldhaus racked up 1,231 points during his four-year career at UK, ranking him thirty-seventh among the program's all-time leading scorers. He also pulled down 540 career rebounds, ranking him forti-eth among all players in that category. During his junior year he led the Wildcats in field-goal percentage, making 52 percent of his attempts.

Feldhaus and teammates Sean Woods, John Pelphrey, and Richie Farmer became known as "The Unforgettables" for remaining with UK after the basketball program was put on NCAA probation during Eddie Sutton's tenure. Then–athletic director C. M. Newton arranged to have their jerseys retired at the end of their senior year.

After a five-year stint playing professional basketball in Japan, Feldhaus returned to Maysville and became an owner of the nine-hole Maysville-based Kenton Station Golf Course, along with his father and stepmother. He teaches golf to local youth and lives in Maysville.

Deron Feldhaus (12), one of "The Unforgettables," followed in the footsteps of his father, Allen Sr., by earning a spot on the Wildcats roster. (Courtesy of the *Lexington Herald-Leader*. Photo by Tim Sharp.)

I can't imagine living anywhere else but Kentucky because all of my family lives in the state. I had opportunities to live elsewhere after college, but I found myself coming back to my hometown of Maysville. The people here are down-home. I'm not a big-city person; I'm more of a country guy, and I love it here.

Playing basketball for UK was my lifelong dream. It's the only program I had ever dreamed of playing for. Growing up I followed every game. I remember the 1978 NCAA Championship Team and James Lee's monster dunks.

My dad, Allen Feldhaus Sr.,[1] was a big influence on me because he had played for Coach Adolph Rupp at UK, and he was my basketball coach at Mason County High School. Dad had also coached my two older brothers: Allen Jr.,[2] who went on to play for Eastern Kentucky University, and Willie,[3] who went on to play for Morehead State University. I think Dad had been a little hard on Allen Jr., but by the time I played for him, I think he realized how to go about coaching one of his sons a little better. The first time that Mason County High School had ever earned a spot in the state high school basketball tournament was during my brother Allen's senior year, in 1981. The team was invited again in 1982, during Willie's junior year. That launched a strong basketball tradition at Mason County High School.

As a coach my dad was demanding. He could put the fear into you so you held a line with him. His coaching style was very precise, especially defensively. I'd put up twelve or fifteen shots a game, but he got everybody on our team involved. He emphasized the importance of taking good shots. Nothing drove him crazier than somebody taking a bad shot. Off the court Dad and I would talk about basketball but never about what happened in one of our games or practices. He'd leave it at the gym. That's the way he wanted it, and that was a benefit, I think. It enabled us to have a good father-son relationship. Today I consider him one of my best friends.

My two brothers also influenced me from the time I was young. Basketball was in their blood. We were competitive like most siblings are, but they constantly challenged me and pushed me to keep up with them, no matter if we were paying basketball, golf, or if we were out frog-catching in water up to our necks. As kids we would build ramps to jump on our bicycles. Often we would approach those ramps from the top of a hill. Before my turn came my brothers would sometimes raise the ramp a few feet without telling me, and I'd go flying! They'd always say, "Come on, Deron, you can do it!" I credit them for making me a strong competitor. Once I got to UK my brothers were my two biggest fans. They made it to every game they could.

My coaches were also supportive. Coach Rick Pitino's drive for hard work impacted me. He did a great job of promoting us and of instilling a sense of confidence in us. More than anything, being a part of the UK program helped build my confidence. That carries me from day to day. Assistant Coach Billy Donovan was almost like one of the players. He was closer to us in age, and sometimes he would practice with us. If I was struggling with something related to basketball, he would help me through it. He could relate to me and my teammates because he had played for Coach Pitino at Providence College.

My teammates and I thought Coach Eddie Sutton was tough on us, but we had no idea how demanding Coach Pitino would be. The NCAA rule limiting a student-athlete's participation to twenty hours a week wasn't in effect during his first year as head coach, so sometimes we would practice three times a day. It was a grind. He didn't have to set curfew because we were worn out. I don't think we had a day off until Christmas that season. The following year, when the NCAA's twenty-hour rule went into effect, we were as happy as could be. But Coach Pitino knew he had to push us for us to be successful. He pushed his coaching staff just as hard.

Another important Kentuckian to me was Mr. Wildcat, Bill Keightley. If I ever arrived early for practice or had free time, I would go in and talk to Mr. Bill. He was somebody you could talk to about anything to get your mind off of things. He was a huge UK basketball fan, but he was more interested in how players were doing in their personal lives, how things were going away from school. He was a caring guy, and he would always ask about my family. That's the way he was with everybody.

My teammate Sean Sutton was also influential. He and I were good friends in high school, were the same age, and we played in state all-star basketball games together. I think my friendship with Sean factored in UK's decision to recruit me.

After my UK career I played professional basketball in Japan for five years. I tried to explain to my teammates and other foreign players there how passionate UK fans are, but it was difficult. You almost have to be a part of it to understand it, I think. UK fans are very knowledgeable. In my opinion the true fans are the ones who sit in the upper levels of Rupp Arena. They're the ones who tune in to call-in shows and who lose sleep when the team loses. They take it to heart.

The first year the UK basketball program was on probation our games were not allowed to be televised. To this day I believe the fans that year were the loudest they'd ever been in Rupp Arena, especially when we won games that we weren't predicted to win. They really embraced us during a season that was supposed to be a low point for the program. Their support was unreal.

Having my jersey retired as a member of "The Unforgettables" was a complete shock. We were not close to the caliber of players that have been honored in that way, but Sean Woods, John Pelphrey, Richie Farmer, and I stuck it out through the down years and helped bring the program back through hard work and dedication. Coach Pitino certainly deserves credit as well. Of course,

I'm probably most remembered for being the guy who was guarding Christian Laettner when he made the game-winning shot that ended our NCAA Tournament run in 1992, but to me, having my jersey retired and hanging from the rafters in Rupp Arena is probably my number-one accomplishment. Every time I walk in to Rupp Arena I look up, and I still can't believe it.

We were not informed beforehand about the unveiling of the jerseys. The night they were unveiled I was sitting next to John Pelphrey on the bench. He pointed up to the four covered jerseys in the rafters and said, "Do you see what I see?"

"No," I replied. "This can't be happening."

21

Travis Ford

Madisonville, Kentucky, native Travis Ford transferred to UK after playing the 1989–1990 season at the University of Missouri, where he averaged 3.5 assists per game. As a Wildcat he was a two-time MVP at the SEC Tournament in 1993 and 1994, and he was named the Southeastern Region MVP as he led UK to the Final Four as a junior in 1994.

An outstanding shooter, Ford ranks sixth all-time in three-point field goals made (190), fourth in three-point field-goal percentage among players with at least 150 attempts (.445), and second in three-point field goals made in a single season (101). He also holds the program's record for highest three-point field-goal percentage with a minimum of one hundred attempts (.529) and for the number of consecutive free throws made (50).

Ford is also tied with Anthony Epps for third place among all-time single-season leaders in assists (193). He led the Wildcats in that category during his junior and senior seasons, having dished out 166 and 193 assists, respectively.

Prior to his current assignment as the head men's basketball coach at Oklahoma State University, Ford was the head coach at Camp-

Travis Ford (5) receives instruction from Coach Rick Pitino. Ford earned
back-to-back Most Valuable Player honors following the SEC Men's
Basketball Tournament in 1993 and 1994. (Courtesy of the *Lexington
Herald-Leader*. Photo by Ron Garrison.)

bellsville University, Eastern Kentucky University, and the University of Massachusetts. He lives in Stillwater, Oklahoma, with his wife, Heather, and their three children, Brooks, Kyleigh, and Shane.

I would not have wanted to grow up anywhere else except in Kentucky, because the state is home to the things that I love and enjoy most in life. My parents, Eddie[1] and Pat Ford, and my sister, Leslie Ford Stuen, live there, as do some of my closest friends. I also enjoy the outdoors, having done so much hunting and fishing growing up in the Bluegrass State. Of course, it's also a basketball state. Kentuckians love their basketball.

I credit my dad for teaching me the game of basketball. He played for Murray State University and went on to become a successful coach at Cuba High School and Webster County High School in Kentucky. He not only taught me the fundamentals of the game, but he taught me how to think the game and to play the game. Dad didn't push basketball on me, but he always provided opportunities for me to be around the game, such as inviting me to come to practice with him or to scout games with him. To this day Dad understands the game as well as anybody I've ever been around.

Don Parson, my coach at Madisonville–North Hopkins High School, was also an important influence on me. He taught me a lot about toughness, and he taught me how to play hard every day. I had a reputation for being one of the better players in the state of Kentucky, but he never was easy on me. He was always very demanding of me, especially early in my high school career. Coach Parson held me responsible and accountable and treated me like everyone else on the team. To this day he's someone I very much admire and respect.

When I transferred to UK after playing my freshman season at the University of Missouri, many people assumed I made the move because Kentucky was my home state and that I had always wanted to play for UK. I was certainly excited for the opportunity to return home and to play for UK, but the main reason was that I wanted to play for Coach Rick Pitino. That was the clincher for me. The fact that he happened to be coaching at UK was icing on the cake, a bonus. I thought his system would be a perfect fit for me. The basketball program had been going through a tough time, and he was building it back up and generating excitement around it. I also knew I wanted to coach someday, and I knew I would learn a lot from him.

Several people influenced me during my career at UK. One was John Pelphrey, who was my roommate for two years. When I arrived I had just finished my freshman year at Missouri. John was beginning his junior year at UK. Not only was he somebody I looked up to and learned a lot from, but he showed me the ropes of the Kentucky basketball program. He also showed me the ropes when it came to playing for Coach Pitino. I looked up to him because I loved his values and the type of person he was—his work ethic, his commitment to the program, and his commitment to the game of basketball. I consider him a close friend to this day.

Assistant Coach Billy Donovan is also somebody I learned a lot from. He was a mentor for me. I remember watching him as a point guard playing when Coach Pitino was head of the basketball program at Providence College. Coach Donovan helped me through a great deal, including some of the pressures of playing for UK and playing for Coach Pitino. He helped me handle some of the difficult times by encouraging me and pulling me to the side to give me advice. He also spent a lot of time individually with me working on my game, especially the year I sat out as a transfer.

My former teammate Jamal Mashburn was another person I really respected. He's one of the nicest people I've ever been around. I enjoyed playing with him because he was such an unselfish player. He made me a much better player. During his junior year he was the number-one player in the country and probably the most unselfish player in the country. I admired his work ethic, and I admired how much he progressed as a player from his freshman year on. I admired how much he grew as a player and as a person.

Coach Pitino's influence on me can't be overestimated. He pushed me to be the best player I could be, motivated me, and taught me so many different things. He put a lot of trust in me as a point guard. Considering that being a college basketball coach is now my profession, there aren't too many major decisions I make these days without running them by Coach Pitino first. I've been the head coach at four different universities, and I've asked for his advice every step of the way. I value his opinion and thoughts as a mentor. He's somebody I talk to as much as possible. What carried over most from my time as a player at UK into my current coaching career was the importance of a strong work ethic and preparing for opponents with scouting reports and the like. We players understood how hard Coach Pitino worked and the time he put into it—the commitment and dedication he had to making our team the best it could be. We knew that nobody was going to outwork him. We knew that we were going to be prepared for every game.

UK basketball is hard to describe unless you played there or unless you're a fan. The fans have a true passion for the game; it's a way of life. They understand the game. A lot of players come to Kentucky but can't handle the pressure, because the pressure is intense when you have such a strong and supportive fan base. I embraced the pressure; I enjoyed it. UK fans don't just cheer you on during your career as a Wildcat; they're loyal fans for a lifetime. There aren't many other fan bases that can compete with UK basketball fans as far as a love for their sport, an understanding of the sport, and a loyal following for a long, long time.

The opportunities I had to play at UK and to play for Coach Pitino brought me a lot of opportunities in life. When you play at

Kentucky you get incredible exposure. You're on a very big stage. I was fortunate to be a member of successful teams at UK that won SEC Championships and competed in a Final Four. That has afforded me a lot of exposure and has helped me along the path of becoming a college basketball coach.

22

Jared Prickett

Fairmont, West Virginia, native Jared Prickett was named the state's "Mr. Basketball" in 1992. At UK the forward was a member of "The Untouchables" team, which won the 1996 NCAA National Championship in a 76–67 contest over Syracuse. He was named to the All-NCAA Regional Team after his freshman season and to the All-SEC Tournament team during his senior season,

Prickett led the Wildcats in rebounding during the 1993–1994 campaign (with 232 rebounds, or an average of 7.0 per game) as well as during the 1996–1997 campaign (with 225 rebounds, or an average of 5.9 per game). He finished his career with 998 points, and he is tied with Saul Smith for fourth place among career leaders in the number of games played (143).

Today Prickett is president and CEO of the Kentucky Basketball Academy. He lives in Lexington with his wife, Kati, and their children, Ryder and Jagger.

Jared Prickett (32) played in five games of the 1995–1996 season before redshirting due to persistent knee pain. (Courtesy of Victoria Graff.)

In 1992 I took my first official recruiting visit with the University of Notre Dame, and I took my second recruiting visit one week later with the University of Kentucky. After my visit to Notre Dame I was ready to sign with them. I come from a small town in West Virginia, and it was amazing to me how beautiful the campus up there was. Then I came to UK. The coaching staff took me to a basketball practice, which was packed with fans and onlookers. I thought, "Wow. This is really nice as well." I returned home and told my dad that I was ready to sign with UK. "Last week you wanted to sign with Notre Dame," he said to me. "What changed?"

UK's assistant coach Herb Sendek is the one who put it in perspective for me during my visit to Lexington. He knew I was leaning toward signing with Notre Dame. "What did you do during your visit there?" Coach Sendek asked. "Go to a football game?"

"Yeah," I said. "It was awesome."

"How much time did you spend in the basketball facility?"

"Probably about thirty minutes," I said.

"When you came to UK, what did you do?"

"I went to a basketball practice."

"Did you see how many people were at the practice?"

"Yes," I said. "It was a lot. They had to turn people away."

Coach Sendek then asked, "Well, what are you going to school to do?"

"I'm going to school to play basketball."

"I know for a fact that people in the state of Kentucky will definitely look out for you," he said. "It's not just one or two people. It's the entire state."

I started digesting that in my mind and became intrigued, so I signed with UK the next Monday.

By June 1992 I was on the UK campus lifting weights, training, and working with my new teammates. I got a bit of a jump start on the other freshmen, which was good for me. You can lift weights as a high school athlete, but it's night and day when you're working with a strength coach at the elite level who's pushing you. I was probably the least-ranked recruit in our class, but mentally I'm probably as tough as you can get.

The entire UK coaching staff had a significant impact on me: Rick Pitino, John O'Brien, Billy Donovan, Herb Sendek, and Winston Bennett. One day Coach Pitino came to practice and started reading from *The Precious Present,* an inspirational book by Dr. Spencer Johnson about the value of being in the moment. The next thing we knew, about two hours had passed, and we hadn't even hit the court. Coach Pitino talked about how we could apply the concepts from that book to our lives on and off the court, advice like "What happened yesterday is finished." And "Learn from your mistakes but then continue moving on and continue getting better." I think everybody responded a little differently to that advice, but I found it practical. For example, you may score twenty points and grab fourteen rebounds in one game, but that game is now in the past. You've got to continue working hard to set yourself up for having more games like that. The opposite is also true. If you have a horrible game with two points and you foul out, that's in the past, too. Just continue working hard.

Coming to UK as a freshman is very difficult because you're used to being "the man" in your high school, with everybody praising you. You might be the best player in the entire state. Then you get to UK, and it brings you down to a reality check. There are other great players on your team, including those who have been lifting weights for a couple of years. They're much stronger than you and a little bit more athletic. Having coaches help you through that transition is important. I think Coach Pitino and the other coaches taught us how to be respectful, grow up, be a man, continue working hard regardless of what's happening, stay positive, and work as a team. All of the coaches were always upbeat and positive, and each one of them has gone on to have their own success, including Billy Donovan, who led the University of Florida to national titles in 2006 and 2007, and our former manager Frank Vogel, who became head coach of the Indiana Pacers. At UK Frank was often in the video room editing tapes, splicing plays so we could understand the other team's offense and defense, so we could get better. So we could win.

Early on in my freshman year I didn't see a lot of playing time, but as the season went on I got to play a little bit more every game. By early February I was starting. During my career I was among the top two or three players in, but most of the time I was a starter. Toward the end of my career Coach Pitino had signed top recruits like Ron Mercer and Antoine Walker. They started immediately, and they got most of the shots. So I became more of a role player: setting picks, rebounding, and staying strong, continuing to earn my minutes. Everybody reaped the rewards of us winning the 1996 national championship. We bought into the system of us being a team and not a group of individuals.

I think the fans liked me because I wasn't the guy coming out there and scoring twenty points every game. I was the guy who did all the intangibles: diving on the floor after the ball, ripping a rebound away from an opponent, or drawing a charge. I was always hustling and trying to be in the right place at the right time. I was also the guy that Coach Pitino yelled at all the time. I learned he was yelling at me because mentally I could take it. That fueled my fire on the court. I think he knew that.

We'd have practices so intense that you'd lose five or seven pounds. I sweat more than most players, so I was often going to Bill Keightley's office to get a new pair of socks and shoes in the middle of practice. I used to call him Wild Bill. He had a little refrigerator stocked with bottled water, soda, and some candy bars and peanut butter crackers. There was nothing special about his office, just a bunch of shoes and socks and practice uniforms.

After my career at UK I played basketball in Europe and in South America until my early thirties. I came back to Lexington and worked a variety of jobs, kind of finding my way. Then in 2009 I became president and CEO of the Kentucky Basketball Academy, a fifty-eight-thousand-square-foot facility with five hardwood basketball courts. Our mission is to provide a focused, structured learning environment while instilling passion, work ethic, and skills in Central Kentucky basketball players, from elite talent to kids who are just learning how to dribble the ball and play the game. I've found what I want to do, and I'm having fun.

23

Jeff Sheppard

A four-year letterman for UK, Marietta, Georgia, native Jeff Sheppard was recruited by Rick Pitino during his career at McIntosh High School in Peachtree City, where he was named Georgia's Player of the Year in 1993.

The guard played on UK's 1996 and 1998 NCAA National Championship teams and was named the 1998 Final Four Most Outstanding Player, scoring sixteen points in the Wildcats' 78–69 victory over Utah.

Sheppard scored 1,091 points during his UK career, which ranks him forty-eighth on the list of the program's all-time leading scorers. He ranks tenth on the list of UK's career leaders in three-point field-goal percentage, having made 128 of his 330 attempts (.3879).

After his UK career Sheppard played eighteen games for the Atlanta Hawks of the NBA, followed by stints with three different pro basketball teams in Italy. He now lives in London, Kentucky, with his wife, Stacey, and their two children. Sheppard is one of the owners of MPC Promotions, a Louisville-based promotional products company.

Guard Jeff Sheppard (15) led the 1997–1998 Wildcats in scoring, averaging 13.7 points per game. (Courtesy of Victoria Graff.)

Bill Keightley, UK's longtime equipment manager, was one of the most influential individuals to me during my four years as a Wildcat. He taught me so many life lessons, primarily by example—how he outworked everybody, how he was prepared for every situation that we faced, how he treated people, how kind and generous he was to everybody he came into contact with. He was a servant to Kentucky basketball. He didn't score any points or get any rebounds, but he is arguably the most influential character in Kentucky basketball history.

I learned a lot from Mr. Keightley's silence in a situation. Before seven o'clock in the morning he knew where all the players and the coaches had been the night before. Some people were where they should have been. Others weren't, but he didn't find that it was necessary to share everything that he knew with everybody in the world. He had an uncanny sense of discretion. He didn't condemn you for anything, and he didn't inflate your ego, either. He also knew how to read people. When high school recruits would come to Lexington he knew right away if they were going to be a good fit or not. He knew who was going to transfer and who wasn't going to make it.

Mr. Keightley's work ethic is probably the thing I appreciate most. To this day I try to work as hard as he did. He was a very early riser. So many people wanted to talk to him and wanted to hang out with him that once eight o'clock in the morning hit, he couldn't get anything done. I see that in my life now. Not that I'm in high demand for my time, but if I can get up early and get two or three good work hours in before people really start coming to work, then I have my most productive days. That was the life Mr. Keightley lived. I never thought I'd miss him as much as I do. Mr. Keightley connected Adolph Rupp with Billy Gillispie. When you lose that connection you lose a lot of perspective on the history of UK basketball. When former players visited Lexington they wouldn't go see the coach or other players. They went to see Mr. Keightley. If you walked into his equipment room you were likely to see Dan Issel, the governor of Kentucky, and Rick Pitino, all laughing about a story that Mr. Keightley was telling. That was the dynamic. There was not a better place in Kentucky to be.

Robert and Jane Fritz of Richmond, Kentucky, are also special people to me. They are the grandparents of one of my high school basketball teammates, Ryan Vickers. When I was still in high school in Georgia, Ryan and I would visit the Fritzes to spend a week fishing and frog gigging. During one of my recruiting visits to UK Robert and Jane invited me to stay at their home in Richmond. In fact, they were the first to know about my decision to sign with UK. During my career at the university they became my grandparents away from home. I would visit them for home-cooked meals, or we would go fishing or frog gigging. They were huge Kentucky fans, but more importantly they took me under their wings and provided me a place to get away from the craziness of being a ball player at Kentucky, a place to relax. They still live in Richmond, and I visit them from time to time.

My wife, the former Stacey Reed, had a big influence on my basketball career and on my life. We met in study hall during my freshman year, but we didn't start to date seriously until a couple of years later. She played on the women's basketball team at UK, so we shared a lot of the same study hall hours, and we were in the same athletic training rooms getting our ankles taped and getting treatments. As a basketball player at UK a lot of people spoil you. They tell you what you want to hear. That can be a bit much for an eighteen- or nineteen-year-old boy. But Stacey was different. She was always brutally honest with me. If I wasn't playing well, she told me so. She told me the truth from day one. I've always appreciated that. We married after college.

Max Appel was another important person to me. At the time

he was the director of the Fellowship of Christian Athletes for Central Kentucky. He held a long-standing Bible study at the Wildcat Lodge. Not every player attended, but Max was there on a consistent basis. He always invited us without any kind of pressure. Out of love he reached out to us and encouraged us. He was always positive, always smiling, always uplifting. A lot of people confided in him. He has an impact on some of the UK basketball players to this day.

I'm forever indebted to Coach Rick Pitino for the opportunity he gave me to play at UK. When you're a high school recruit it's easy to think that everybody should be offering you a scholarship. But when you grow older and you reflect on how many scholarships there are, and how the timing of positions has to work out, you really appreciate falling into one of those coveted scholarships. I learned so many things from Coach Pitino on the basketball court that I use today, including the importance of a strong work ethic and being well prepared, but perhaps the biggest thing I learned from him was how to say "thank you." In December 2012 I met with Coach Pitino and thanked him for providing me the opportunity to play at Kentucky. I don't think I'd ever told him so before. I came to realize that many of us former college athletes don't return thanks to those who give us that opportunity. We should, because it's a privilege to be a student-athlete, especially at UK. During my visit with Coach Pitino we reflected on our teams. We had some tremendous teams, arguably one of the best runs in college basketball history. There were tremendous margins of victory, a style of play that changed how basketball is played with the three-point line, as well as his aggressive trapping and full-court defenses.

In recent years I have spent a lot of time with my former teammates from the 1996 NCAA National Championship team. We're appreciative of our run. We look back now at how difficult it is to be in the mix for a national title year after year. It doesn't happen much anymore. Guys are leaving early for the NBA, and there's not a solid transition from one team to the next. Continuity was a huge part of our lives when I played at UK. We spent a lot of time with each other during the off-season, got to know each other, and had a lot of fun together. We competed at a really high level against each other and pushed each other. The result was a really strong team dynamic that was difficult for opponents to break.

The current situation of "one and done" players in college basketball is unfortunate because the athlete who stays for his college career is almost penalized. In the eyes of the NBA, if you don't leave early, then something must be wrong. It's a different era now. Maybe it will change and there will be another wave where players will choose to stay in college longer, or maybe not. It definitely has helped the parity in college basketball, though. It's allowed schools like Butler University and Virginia Commonwealth University to make impressive runs in the NCAA Tournament. It's made it more difficult for the powerhouse schools to dominate the landscape of college basketball.

There is an interesting dynamic with UK fans who are born and raised in the Bluegrass State. They display a phenomenal love for Kentucky basketball and an extraordinary disdain for archrivals Louisville, Duke, and Indiana. Even though I played at UK I don't have that same level of distaste for our rival opponents that people like my wife and daughter do, because I was not born in Kentucky. They were. For example, Coach Pitino now coaches the Louisville Cardinals. I cheer for his team, but my daughter can't stand it. She gets upset with me. My wife is the same way.

I've met Louisville fans who feel the same way about UK. I do a lot of work in Louisville, and I try to be diplomatic when I encounter diehard Cardinals fans with statements like, "Can't we just all get along? Can't we cheer for one another?" Often the reply is "No way!" There is something bred into basketball fans who are born in Kentucky: they're either devoted to UK or devoted to Louisville.

From the fans' standpoint UK basketball is larger than Coach Adolph Rupp, Coach Pitino, Coach John Calipari, or any All-American who has played there. They cheer for UK basketball, not for any one person. It is what they talk about, cheer about, cry about, and whine about. The fans refer to themselves as "we." They'll say things like, "We're not rebounding the ball enough." They may live in Pikeville and have nothing to do with the rebounding during a game going on at Rupp Arena in downtown Lexington, but they consider themselves a part of the program. They are.

24

Allen Edwards

Recruited by Rick Pitino while at Miami (Florida) Senior High School, Allen Edwards played a reserve role behind Tony Delk on UK's 1996 national championship team, which defeated Syracuse 76–67. Two years later, Edwards's senior season, he was one of three captains on UK's 1998 national championship team, which defeated Utah 78–69. He finished his senior year averaging a career-best 9.2 points, 3.3 assists, and 3.3 rebounds per game.

After UK Edwards played in both the Continental Basketball Association and the International Basketball Association before returning to UK in 2002 to complete his college degree and to serve as a special assistant to Tubby Smith during the 2002–2003 campaign.

Prior to being hired as an assistant coach for the University of Wyoming men's basketball team in 2011, Edwards held assistant coaching stints at Western Kentucky University, Towson University, Virginia Commonwealth University, and Morehead State University.

Edwards married his college sweetheart, LaTanya Webb, who played volleyball at UK. They have two daughters, Mai'a and Landree, and a son, Jaxson. The family lives in Laramie, Wyoming.

Allen Edwards is the younger brother of Doug Edwards, a basketball star at Florida State University who went on to play in the NBA, and Steve Edwards, who played basketball for the Miami Hurricanes. (Courtesy of *The Cats' Pause*.)

As a high school recruit at Miami Senior High School in Florida, I developed a good relationship with UK's assistant coach Billy Donovan and head coach Rick Pitino. During the open period for college coaches to be out on the recruiting trail, it felt like one of them was always in the stands to see me play. That made an impression on me and separated them from other programs. I also heard good things about UK and the fan base from Gimel Martinez, a predecessor of mine at Miami Senior High School who played for UK, as well as from some of my high school teammates who had played in tournaments held in Memorial Coliseum. Another factor in my decision to sign with UK was that I really wanted to get out of the state of Florida. I wanted to get away from home, see something different, and kind of grow up. In fact, I made my decision to sign with UK even before taking my official visit there. That's how comfortable I was with the situation. It just felt right.

It's difficult to pinpoint a specific person of great influence on me during my time at UK, but I will say that the general bond that I had with my teammates was strong. I had the pleasure of getting to know all the guys I played with. I wasn't part of a clique, so to speak. I was an even-keeled kid who got along with everybody, though my former college roommates are the ones I keep in touch with the most: Antoine Walker and Nazr Mohammed. Scott Padgett and I also remain good friends. I remember arriving in Kentucky for my freshman year before school started and staying with Scott's family for a few days before we had to be in Lexington, so I got to know his mother and father. I also learned from the upperclassmen on our team. I thought Tony Delk, Walter McCarty, and Mark Pope were tremendous in setting the right examples for us younger guys.

In addition to my coaches and teammates, many different people helped me through my four years at UK. Ted and Barbara Faulconer of Lancaster, Kentucky, were like host parents to me. I got to know them during my freshman year. They reached out when I wasn't playing much and befriended me. Barbara always baked me oatmeal raisin cookies on my birthday. I thought it was a kind gesture, and our friendship grew from there. In fact, the Faulconers attended my wedding, and they were in the hospital for the arrival of my firstborn child. They always send a Christmas card and a birthday card to my wife and each of our three kids, and to this day Barbara still sends me oatmeal raisin cookies on my birthday. She and Ted continue to check in on me and follow my coaching career.

C. B. Akins Sr., pastor of First Baptist Bracktown in Lexington, was also helpful. I first met Pastor Akins during my senior year at UK. It was a small church at the time, the kind where they would seat you in the pulpits if it got too crowded. I sat in one of the pulpits for the service and had the opportunity to meet Pastor Akins afterward. A week or two later my mother, Laura Mae Edwards, passed away. Soon after I arrived home in Miami from Lexington to be with family, my aunt picked up the phone and told me that my pastor was on the line.

"My pastor?" I said. "I don't have a pastor."

When I picked up the phone, it was Pastor Akins. I appreciated him reaching out to me with support. From that point on we developed a good relationship, and I attended church more. To this day, when I'm close to Lexington I make an effort to stop by church to see him.

Another important person to me was Father Ed Bradley,[1] who was UK's team chaplain. He sat on the end of our bench during games and was tremendous in the sense of bringing a nature of peace around us. He was always so friendly and loving.

Sheila Breeding, my academic advisor, went over and beyond regular work hours to help me from an educational standpoint, sometimes until midnight or two o'clock in the morning. She was always adamant about my earning my degree and made sure I was doing what I needed to do to be successful. She took that same approach with numerous student-athletes.

I don't think there is another love affair in college sports like there is between the UK basketball program and the Big Blue Nation fan base, with the possible exception of University of Alabama football and its fans. I think every true-blue Kentucky fan is not only a fan but a coach. They'll spend inordinate amounts of time scouting out the competition prior to the team's next game. You see this during the SEC Tournament, where there are typically more UK fans in the stands for matchups of other teams in the conference than fans of the teams actually competing against each other.

An incident that occurred after we won the 1998 national championship put the passion of Big Blue Nation fans in perspective for me. It was my senior year, and I was touring the state with my teammates Jeff Sheppard and Cameron Mills to sign autographs. We were at a session at Fayette Mall in Lexington, where we had agreed to sign autographs for two hours. The line was so long that it went past the two hours, so the three of us agreed to stay an extra hour. Even after that extra hour there was still a long line! At that point the event organizers cut the line off and told people that was the end of the signing. People started to cry. Not just kids. Adults cried. I was in awe. I don't know if another hour would have been sufficient to sign all those autographs, but to see all those people react like that was unbelievable to me.

The experiences and success I enjoyed at UK playing for Coach Pitino and Coach Smith benefited me in terms of how I carry myself and the demeanor I possess as a college basketball coach, but not just in terms of teaching the game and carrying out my current responsibilities as an assistant coach for the University of Wyoming Cowboys. The other part is the importance of getting to know the kids on our team. There's an old saying that rings true with me: "A kid is not going to care how much you know about basketball until he understands how much you care about him." You have to spend time with kids away from basketball to help cultivate your relationship with them. When you cultivate that relationship, you can get more out of them on the floor because they understand that it's not just about basketball. They understand that you care about them as a person.

25

Derek Anderson

During his senior year at Louisville's Doss High School in 1992, Derek Anderson was named a Kentucky High School Basketball All-Star and was a finalist for that year's "Mr. Basketball" honors in the state. The guard played at Ohio State for two years before transferring to UK, where he redshirted the 1995 season.

At UK Anderson ranks second all-time behind Rajon Rondo in steals per game (a 1.782-per-game average), and he ranks sixth all-time in three-point field-goal percentage among players who made at least 150 attempts (.3987). He scored eleven points in the 1996 NCAA National Championship game, which UK won over Syracuse 76–67.

After earning a degree in pharmacy from UK in 1997, Anderson was selected by the Cleveland Cavaliers as the thirteenth overall pick in the NBA draft and went on to play for six other NBA teams, including the Miami Heat during its 2006 NBA Championship season. He finished his eleven-year NBA career averaging twelve points per game, 3.2 rebounds per game, and 3.4 assists per game.

In the summer of 2013 Anderson returned to UK to complete a minor in social work. Today he is a screenwriter, film producer, and

Derek Anderson was named a cocaptain of the 1996–1997 Wildcats team his senior year. (Courtesy of Victoria Graff.)

book author who maintains homes in Los Angeles and Atlanta. He is
also president of the Derek Anderson Foundation, which supports dis-
advantaged youth.

As a child growing up in Louisville I had no real family to speak
of. My mother was a substance abuser, and my dad left us, so by
the time I was eleven I was on my own. Homeless people ignored
me and literally walked over top of me. A lot of people didn't want
to help me, so I lived in shelter homes. I had no idea of what family was.

During my senior year of high school my uncle, George Williams, allowed me to stay with him after he learned I had been sleep-
ing in so many different people's homes, including that of a high
school coach of mine. Uncle George taught me how to be a man. He
taught me responsibility and how to get a job. I had a son I had to
pay child support for at age fourteen, so he made sure I developed,
and he made sure I stayed focused.

Outside of Uncle George and my son, Derek Jr., I had no real
family until I came to UK as a transfer in 1995. There I learned
that people really cared about me. Wherever I went on campus,
whether it was to the dining hall or to the bookstore, people
treated me like I was a member of their family. They struck up
conversations with me and showed concern. There were so many
people who impacted me. It wasn't just a few people I considered
as brothers and sisters; I loved all of them. There was nothing there
but love, and I've always looked at it that way. That's why I'm so
dedicated to UK now.

During my three years at Kentucky everyone I came in contact with had a say-so in the things that happened to me: my teammates, coaches, the secretaries, the ball boys, and the managers all
became family. We all knew our managers and ball boys by name.

It was a focal point for us. How many players at universities today can say that?

The bond I formed with my teammates was special. We'd go to movies and bowling together; we did everything together. They were like my brothers. Tony Delk just called me today to tell me he was coming to town. That's the rule: whenever one of us is in the other one's city, we call. Whenever I'm in Nashville I call Ron Mercer. We're all still connected because we made that bond in college.

Coach Rick Pitino gave all of us an opportunity to play. That's all you can ask from a coach: "Give me an opportunity, and let me make the most out of it." The assistant coaches Delray Brooks and Winston Bennett did their part, too. They studied, they were focused, and they taught us. I really appreciated that.

When you become an NCAA champion like our team did in 1996, you're a champion for life. You understand the value of it. But when you're playing basketball just for the sake of playing, it's easy to lose focus. For example, if you're in a relationship with someone but you don't do anything to nurture it and make it grow, it becomes nothing more than a relationship; it's not a friendship. The members of our 1996 team cared about each other as people, and it showed. That's why we were always so successful. We did more than just play basketball, but we were always competitive with each other. For example, the day after we won the championship game, we were on our way back home to Lexington and started some friendly trash-talking among ourselves. The second-string players were saying things to the starting players like, "You guys would not have won that game without us." It was a friendly debate, but it was decided that when we got home we'd meet up in Memorial Coliseum to compete against each other. We took to the court around 11:00 p.m., and we stopped after a while because guys started to play too rough with one another. It was getting physical. Then we just started laughing and joking around.

Playing basketball for UK is like being part of a large family-owned company: you're the son, and you have to keep the family business going, the tradition going. It's almost like it's bred in people to keep the company going, and they're all in the same business of winning. That's how I view Kentucky basketball. Most everyone who's a fan is born into it. There are very few that we have to convert.

There is no other fan support like that of the Big Blue Nation. When I tore my anterior cruciate ligament (ACL) during my senior year in 1997, those fans were there for me. I probably received three thousand get-well cards from fans when that happened. Fast-forward to early 2013, when I did a signing for my book, *Stamina*, at a Lexington bookstore. I gave about a week's notice that I was coming, and close to six hundred people showed up! That was amazing to me.

On February 12, 2013, I was at home in Atlanta watching the UK-Florida matchup on TV and saw UK freshman Nerlens Noel go down with a torn ACL. I felt awful for him, and I flashed back to the two times I tore my own ACL: once at Ohio State University and once at UK. I was away from my team. I felt alone. Some nights were miserable, sitting in my dorm room thinking, "Am I ever going to make it as a basketball player? What if I don't make it? Who would help me out? What if things don't work out the way I want them to work out?" It was a really sad day in my life. I knew that when Nerlens got injured he was mentally going to feel the exact same way: alone. I thought to myself, "This kid's going to need me." Other people who've never been alone wouldn't understand that. They've always had parents or someone to make them feel better. Growing up I never had that luxury, so I know what it feels like to be truly alone. I didn't want Nerlens to feel that way, so I packed a suitcase, and the next morning I flew to Lexington to meet with him. I had only met Nerlens once briefly before, but I wanted to make sure he knew there was someone supporting him and that he would not have to go through the injury, the surgery, and the rehab alone.

When I arrived in Lexington Nerlens was open and receiving, and he was excited that I made the trip to see him. He had been watching some highlights from my playing days, and he said, "You recovered from two torn ACLs, and you were still dunking on people!" I told him, "See? You can make it."

There is no one person who's made it in life without help from a group of people. Bill Gates needed other people to build Microsoft and be successful. I consider the people at UK as being the first real family that I've ever had, and they continue to help me build who I am.

26

Orlando ("Tubby") Smith

*Tubby Smith was no stranger to UK when he was named head coach in
1997. He had been an assistant coach on Rick Pitino's staff from 1989 to
1991, before subsequent head-coaching stints at the University of Tulsa
and the University of Georgia.*

*In his first year as UK's head coach, Smith guided the 1997–1998
Wildcats to the program's seventh NCAA National Championship, with
a 78–69 victory over Utah.*

*During his ten-year tenure Smith averaged almost twenty-six
wins per season, and he guided UK to five SEC regular-season championships, five SEC Tournament titles, six Sweet Sixteen finishes, and four
Elite Eight finishes. He won the Naismith College Coach of the Year in
2003 and the Jim Phelan Coach of the Year in 2005.*

*After a six-year stint as head men's basketball coach at the Uni-
versity of Minnesota, Smith was hired by Texas Tech University in April
2013 to lead its men's basketball program. He and his wife, Donna,
have three sons: G. G., who was named the head coach of Loyola University Maryland in April 2013; Saul, who played guard at UK during his father's tenure and was an assistant coach at the University of*

During his ten-year tenure, Tubby Smith guided UK to one national championship, five SEC Tournament titles, and six Sweet Sixteen finishes. (Courtesy of Victoria Graff.)

Minnesota; and Brian, who is the head boys' basketball coach at Rancho Solano Private Schools in Peoria, Arizona.

My first connection to the University of Kentucky came about because of Charles Martin ("C. M.") Newton,[1] UK's former athletic director, who became an important mentor to me. I first met Coach Newton when he was head coach of the Vanderbilt Commodores men's basketball team. At that time I was an assistant coach for the University of South Carolina Gamecocks. Our head coach was George Felton,[2] who allowed me to do a lot, in particular coaching our team defense.

During the 1986–1987 season the Gamecocks upset the Commodores, and our team did a great defensive job. Center Will Perdue[3] played on that team, and they were in the top twenty at the time. After the game I remember Coach Felton introducing me to Coach Newton as our team's defensive coach, and I think Coach Newton remembered that encounter, because after he became athletic director at UK in 1989, Coach Newton and Stu Jackson[4] recommended me to Coach Rick Pitino for an assistant coach position. I tell my players all the time that you don't get a second chance to make a first impression. I didn't really know Rick Pitino at the time, but I knew Stu Jackson, who had been on Rick's coaching staff at Providence College.

After Rick Pitino left UK in 1997 to coach the Boston Celtics, Coach Newton hired me as the program's head coach. I remember him saying, "We're going to pay you well here, Tubby, but you're going to earn every penny." And he was right. He emphasized doing things first-class and the right way. His office was down the hall from mine, so we were close. Coach Newton has helped guide me in my career and continues to play an important role in my life.

Another influential person to me was Bill Keightley, the basketball program's longtime equipment manager. He provided support and always put Kentucky basketball in perspective for me. There was no one more loyal or who loved UK basketball more than Bill Keightley. He'd been the equipment manager for forty-eight years, and I don't remember him ever missing a day. He'd be there at five o'clock in the morning, every day. An ex-marine, he represented loyalty, commitment, and dedication. Win or lose, you knew he was going to say the right things to you and to the team. He had a way of making you feel better. Bill would often say to me and to the players, "Boy, I never worked a day in my life. This is just too much fun to be work."

One of his common phrases was "don't tighten up, lighten up," which he would say when things were tense or before big matchups like the games with the University of Louisville.

Marta McMackin also had a real influence on me because she had been at UK since the 1970s as an administrative assistant to my predecessors Rick Pitino, Eddie Sutton, and Joe B. Hall. She showed me the lay of the land and protected me in so many ways. Marta knew who the movers and the shakers were in UK athletics, at the university, and in the Big Blue Nation. Everybody wants a piece of the head coach at Kentucky, and you can wear yourself out by obligating yourself too much. Early in my tenure she would say, "This person is important to talk to, Coach," and she would also be the one that was able to say "no" to requests for my time or involvement. I'm not a guy who can easily say "no."

It's amazing to me how many people's lives are touched and influenced by UK basketball. It's something they really hang their hats on. The program has eight NCAA National Championships now, which is an amazing feat. The fans are loyal and grateful. Even today, when I walk through an airport, UK fans will stop me and say, "Coach, we appreciate what you did." But the truth is, I appreciate them as much as they appreciate me. I can promise you that.

As a coach, you love the fans, and you want their support. Having an affinity for the fan base is essential. You are providing a service coaching their team. You are trying to win, and you are trying to do the right things for your players, your coaches, the university, and the fans. Fans may boo you or cheer you. They call and they write with praise and criticism. But you can't let that affect you, or you're not going to last long in coaching or be successful in coaching. I became a college coach for the student-athletes, to get them educated and to teach them the game of basketball.

During my tenure at UK there was an element of the fan base that didn't think our teams had won enough games, but in five of my ten years as coach we probably played the toughest schedules in the history of UK basketball. I wish we could have won more games while I was head coach. But we were competitive, we graduated our players, and we kept the program clean. If there was pressure, it was pressure to make sure we did things in a first-class manner.

One thing I appreciate about UK fans is that they know how to be grateful, because the program has been so successful, and the fans are proud of that success. They show their pride, and they should. They show their commitment by calling in to talk shows, writing letters, and flocking to Rupp Arena or wherever the team plays. You're not going to find more loyal, passionate fans for their team than followers of the Wildcats. That's the one common thing. Just about everybody in Kentucky is pulling for you to be successful. It's a way of life in the Commonwealth.

27

Marquis Estill

A three-year letter winner at UK, Richmond, Kentucky, native Marquis Estill was named the 1999 Gatorade State Player of the Year after his senior year at Madison Central High School, averaging 20.5 points and 11.3 rebounds per game.

At UK Estill scored 936 points, and he ranks ninth all-time in the number of blocks made (143, or an average of 1.4 per game). He was named Second Team All-SEC in 2003, his junior season, while also earning All-NCAA Regional team honors, as well as SEC All-Tournament team honors. That same year he led the Wildcats in field-goal percentage by making 62.4 percent of his shot attempts. He finished his UK career as the program's all-time leader in field-goal percentage among players with at least four hundred attempts (.6013).

Estill served as an undergraduate assistant on John Calipari's staff at UK during the 2012–2013 basketball season. He lives in Lexington with his wife, Emily, and their two children, Eli and Isla.

Marquis Estill is UK's career leader in field-goal percentage among players with at least four hundred shot attempts (.6013). (Courtesy of *The Cats' Pause*.)

My mom, Tanya Smith, had a big impact on me. You always want to make your mother happy. She was a great mother, a single mother who raised two boys on her own and adopted my cousin, Yolanda, who became my sister. She and my grandmother, Patricia Farris, did an outstanding job taking care of us, making sure we had everything that we needed. They also did a great job helping me keep my head on straight and keeping me away from people I wanted to hang around who were getting into trouble. I wanted to do the right thing for them. They were probably my biggest role models.

Having grown up in Kentucky it meant a lot to me and my family to have the opportunity to play basketball at UK. Some of my relatives really wanted me to play for the University of Louisville. As a recruit I was considering UK, Louisville, the University of Tennessee, and the University of Alabama at Birmingham. When I came to UK on my recruiting visit I was impressed with how the players treated me. It was like one big family. Everybody was hanging out together; they were like brothers. That's what I was used to in high school with my teammates. It felt like it was the same at UK, and I wanted to be a part of that. Plus, a lot of people back home in Richmond didn't think I could play for UK. I was overweight and out of shape. That gave me more reason to come here and show people what I could really do.

Coach Tubby Smith was like a father figure to me. He gave me great advice throughout the years and made sure I stayed on the right path. I remember him telling me, "You can be the best post player that I ever coached. You just have to work hard." That motivated me to get better. I was fifty pounds overweight when I arrived at UK as a freshman. I busted my tail that summer, lost fifty pounds, and got down to playing weight.

David Kindy, the former athletic trainer at UK, was also important to me. I had two knee surgeries in high school and two more during my career at UK. Dave was like a brother to me. He did everything he could to make my knees feel good. He put so much time and effort into trying to make me be able to play basketball, and I'm thankful for all he did. I used to be in the training room with him for hours before practice and after practice, as early as 6:00 a.m. sometimes. During my junior year Dave came up with a special training regimen, and my knees felt brand-new. I played through that whole season without any knee problems.

Former Wildcat Nazr Mohammed was another influence. I used to watch him play when I was in high school. When he came to UK he was also overweight. He and I have similar body types. When I arrived at UK during the summer of my freshman year, he was on campus working out. He recommended a dietary plan for me to go by, and he shared the workouts that helped him lose weight. We're still friends to this day.

The support from UK fans is nothing short of great. They stick with you no matter what. They care about you off the court, not just on the court. It makes you work hard for them, when you have such a big crowd that supports you, comes to all your games, and cheers for you. That definitely motivated me as a player. During my sophomore year I had a big game against North Carolina, with nineteen points and eleven rebounds. I didn't play well in the next game, so I was on the bench. It was a home game. The crowd started chanting my nickname: "Quis! Quis! Quis! We want Quis!" It really got loud. I finally got called in to enter the game. I went in there and played well. That was a great moment for me, to hear the fans calling out my name because they wanted me in the game.

Before my aunt Ronetta Farris passed away in 2003 I promised her that I would return to UK and finish my bachelor's degree. I earned that degree in May 2013, in agriculture and community and leadership development. This came on the heels of having the opportunity to serve on Coach John Calipari's staff as an undergraduate assistant coach during the 2012–2013 basketball season. That was

a great experience. These coaches put in a lot of work. Most players really don't understand the time and the effort that coaches put
into making the practice schedules, breaking down film, and going
over every player's tendencies. When you're a player it's easy to take
things for granted. You don't always respect what coaches really do
to make you a better player and try to help you reach your goals and
be successful. In my role as an assistant coach I tried to teach the
players to do the right things on and off the court, mainly off the
court. My advice to them was simple: as long as you have a good
career here, once you get done playing ball, you're going to be taken
care of. Somebody's always going to be willing to help you out if you
do the right things and stay out of trouble.

Part IV

The 2000s–2010s

On December 8, 2001, with a 79–59 victory over the University of North Carolina Tar Heels, UK became the first program in college basketball history to reach eighteen hundred wins. Two years later Tubby Smith guided the Wildcats to a 19–0 sweep of SEC opponents, a fitting way to mark the basketball program's one-hundred-year anniversary. At the end of the 2007 campaign Smith resigned from UK, accepting an offer to become head coach of the University of Minnesota Gophers. He left the program with a 263–83 record (76 percent), having averaged twenty-six wins per season during his ten-year tenure, including a 29–13 record in NCAA Tournament play.

On April 6, 2007, UK named former Texas A&M coach Billy Gillispie as head coach. Despite Gillispie's having landed heralded recruit Patrick Patterson from Huntington, West Virginia, his tenure was short-lived. He compiled an overall record of 40–27 in two seasons (60 percent) before being fired by UK on March 27, 2009—during a season in which the Wildcats failed to make an NCAA Tournament bid for the first time since 1991.

On April 1, 2009, UK named former University of Massachusetts and University of Memphis coach John Calipari as the program's twenty-second head coach. Early in his tenure UK became the first program in college basketball history to reach two thousand wins, with an 88–44 victory over Drexel University on December 21, 2009. The team sported "UK2K" t-shirts after the victory.

What the Wildcats achieved during Calipari's first three seasons was transformative. UK finished the 2009–2010 campaign with an overall record of 35–3, falling 66–73 to the West Virginia Mountaineers in the Elite Eight on March 27, 2010. Along the way the Wildcats had been ranked number one and had earned both the SEC Championship and the SEC Tournament title. Five players from that year's roster were selected in the first round of the 2010 NBA draft—a first for any college program.

The 2010–2011 squad achieved an overall record of 29–9, falling 55–56 to the Connecticut Huskies in the Final Four on April 2, 2011. Four players from that roster were selected in the 2011 NBA draft.

The following year's team began the season with a number-one ranking and ended the campaign with a 38–2 record, culminating in UK's eighth NCAA national title, a 67–59 victory over the University of Kansas Jayhawks on April 2, 2012. Six players from that year's roster were selected in the 2012 NBA draft, including number-one pick Anthony Davis, an exceptional shot-blocker who finished the season with numerous honors, including the National Player of the Year, the SEC Player of the Year, and the 2012 NCAA Tournament Most Outstanding Player.

Even though Calipari landed a top-ranked recruiting class for the fourth season in a row, the 2012–2013 squad struggled with consistency and was dealt a setback when star freshman Nerlens Noel suffered a season-ending torn ACL injury during a matchup at the University of Florida on February 12, 2013. The Wildcats finished the season with a 21–12 record and failed to earn a bid for the NCAA Tournament. UK lost to Robert Morris 59–57 in the first round of National Invitational Tournament play.

28

Chuck Hayes

A four-year letterman for UK, San Leandro, California, native Chuck Hayes was recruited by Tubby Smith during his career at Modesto Christian High School, where he was named the state's "Mr. Basketball" in 2001.

A forward, Hayes scored 1,211 points during his career as a Wildcat, which ranks him fortieth on the list of the program's all-time leading scorers. He also ranks seventh all-time in rebounds (910) and eighth all-time in steals (170).

Hayes led UK in rebounding during three consecutive seasons (an average of 6.8 per game, 8.1 per game, and 7.7 per game during 2002–2003, 2003–2004, and 2004–2005, respectively) and in free-throw percentage during three seasons (.738, .788, and .730 during 2001–2002, 2002–2003, and 2004–2005, respectively). He also led the 2003–2004 squad with 45 blocks, for an average of 1.4 per game.

After a five-year stint with the NBA's Houston Rockets Hayes joined the Sacramento Kings roster in December 2011. In 2013 Hayes was traded to the Toronto Raptors. He lives with his son, Dorian Titus Hayes.

Chuck Hayes was named the 2005 SEC Defensive Player of the Year. He also earned All-SEC honors in 2004 and 2005. (Courtesy of Victoria Graff.)

Before I arrived at UK fans did not know a lot about me because I had played high school basketball in California, and I wasn't a big-time recruit. But once I stepped on the court to play for UK, the people of Kentucky embraced me, welcomed me, and took me in as their own. The southern accent of people in the state took some getting used to, but all of the relationships I created there made Kentucky a second home for me. When I first visited as a recruit I was impressed by how close Lexington was to so many other destinations. By car you can get to Cincinnati in about one hour and a half and to Indianapolis in about three and a half hours—everything is so close.

There are five people from my time at Kentucky whom I hold close to this day, starting with my former head coach, Tubby Smith. He's a great man. I admire everything about him: his morals, his beliefs, and his unselfishness. Coach Smith has supported me throughout my career. Whenever I was out on the basketball court for UK, it was like I was representing him; I represented his beliefs and his coaching style. That's why I played as hard as I did. Coach Smith referred to me as a "warrior," and I take that as a compliment. These days, I send him birthday wishes, and he sends me mine. We get together for dinner when we can. When he coached at the University of Minnesota, he often came to see me play when the Sacramento Kings matched up with the Minnesota Timberwolves in Minneapolis.

Two other people close to me from my time at UK are my former teammates Josh Carrier and Ravi Moss. Josh and I arrived at UK in the same freshman class, so we formed an automatic bond. As sophomores Josh and I kind of "adopted" Ravi, who was part of the incoming freshman class. Both Ravi's family and Josh's family invited me to every holiday that I couldn't make it home to California. They took me in like a member of their own family. Now my son and Ravi's son are exactly a month apart in age, so our kids are growing up together even though we're so far apart geographically. I was in Josh's wedding two years ago. The relationship I have with those guys is special. I talk to them just about every day, and whenever we see each other in person it's like a family reunion.

Another important person to me during my time at UK was Leon Smith, who was the director of men's basketball operations. He was a mentor to me, Josh, and Ravi off the court in terms of how to carry ourselves on campus and throughout the city of Lexington. His office door was always open for us, whether we wanted to talk about something related to basketball or related to our lives off the court. We often turned to him for advice. Mandy Polley, now Mandy Brajuha, UK's former assistant media relations director, also looked out for me, Josh, and Ravi. She was like a protective sister to us. She wanted to know who we were dating, who we were talking to, if they were good for us, and who to watch out for. Those five people really helped me during my college experience.

As a player, some of my most memorable moments occurred during the annual Southeastern Conference men's basketball tournament. Every SEC school is represented in that tournament, so the stands are full of fans wearing the colors of their favorite SEC school. But the UK fans who came to that tournament always outnumbered fans from other SEC schools, and, at least to me, they created a different energy in the way they supported us, whether we had a good game or a bad game. It didn't matter; they had our backs. They showed me so much encouragement when I was out on the court. Even during the regular season UK fans pack every game. If they can't make it to the home games they'll make it to away games. It doesn't matter where the Cats travel to: Big Blue Nation will be there. That separates us. We're everywhere.

I try to visit Kentucky every summer to see friends, to reminisce, and to share stories. Everything I learned from the people I mentioned, from the reception I received from UK fans, and from the lessons I've learned throughout college, 1 apply in everyday life. I hope to pass along these same lessons to my son and try to teach him a thing or two.

29

Ravi Moss

Hopkinsville, Kentucky, native Ravi Moss started at the guard position all four years at University Heights High School. As a senior he averaged twenty-one points per game and ten rebounds per game, earning second-team all-state honors from the Louisville Courier-Journal *and honorable-mention all-state recognition from the* Lexington Herald-Leader.

As a walk-on at UK, Moss was known for his defensive hustle and for coming off the bench and hitting big shots. He scored nineteen points and grabbed six rebounds during UK's 83–79 loss to North Carolina in Rupp Arena on December 5, 2005. UK was ranked number ten in the nation at the time.

Moss earned All-Academic SEC honors during his freshmen, sophomore, junior, and senior years. He is currently a sales representative for AstraZeneca Pharmaceuticals. He and his son, Braylon, live in Lexington.

Ravi Moss was a member of UK teams that won the SEC Tournament title twice (in 2003 and 2004) and reached the Elite Eight twice (in 2003 and 2005). (Courtesy of Victoria Graff.)

The University of Kentucky is the institution Kentuckians most strongly identify with. That was a big part of my decision to walk on at UK, because the university is so respected by people in the state. Even citizens who don't attend or graduate from UK consider it "their school." That's how they identify themselves. Understanding that and learning that at such a young age made it even more special when I earned a spot on the basketball team as a walk-on. It also meant so much because I had grown up watching all the players Rick Pitino had recruited and coached. I attended summer basketball camps at UK and got to meet and interact with players like Anthony Epps, Derek Anderson, and Antoine Walker. They were my coaches during the summer. As soon as I arrived on campus as a player one of the first people I saw was Anthony Epps. He gave me a big hug of congratulations. We're still close friends.

During my freshman year I was struggling. I would measure myself against the best of the best—guys like my teammates Keith Bogans and Gerald Fitch—but at the time I was frustrated. I was playing as hard as I could, and they were just better than me. I was ready to quit the team, but the director of basketball operations, Leon Smith, talked me off the edge. I'd say things like, "I'm not good enough to be here" and "I don't think I can do this." He said, "No. Give it time. Stick it out; you'll be fine."

Another person who deserves credit for my development as a player is Assistant Coach Dave Hobbs. He was one of the first people to push for me to get more playing time. He spent extra time with me working on my shot mechanics, and he helped me build confidence in myself. For example, I was playing pick-up games with my teammates, but I felt out of my league. They were all so much better than I was, but Coach Hobbs would watch our pick-up games every now and then. He recognized that I was getting picked in the first game most of the time. "That means something," he told me. "You might not understand it now, but you've got game. You can play; you've just got to believe in yourself."

Although I didn't play a lot of minutes during my freshman year, our 2002–2003 team was awesome. We won twenty-six games in a row, went 16–0 in the SEC, and went 32–4 overall. I grew so much as a player because of what Coach Hobbs did. I give him credit for most of my career because he gave me the tools and the confidence to really go for it and believe that I could play at a high level. I did a lot of individual workouts with him. I would stay sometimes an hour or an hour and a half after practice, just shooting. He stayed there with me until I got the ball into the right position and my elbow into the right position. He definitely went above and beyond what most people would do, and I really appreciated that.

I formed strong bonds with my teammates Chuck Hayes and Josh Carrier. They were one year ahead of me, but I count them as my best friends to this day. In college, Josh's dorm room was the place to be. He had a PlayStation, a sound system, a computer, and he had the most comfortable couch. I don't know how many naps we had there. We got along great.

After our team lost to Michigan State University in the double-overtime Elite Eight game on March 27, 2005, in Austin, Texas, I was devastated not just because we lost a chance to advance to the Final Four but because I was losing Josh and Chuck as teammates, too. They were seniors and our team captains, so that was their final game in a UK uniform. I remember the flight home from that game. We were on a big plane, and I had a row of seats to myself. Chuck sat across the aisle from me in another row of seats. I kept looking over at him, and I pretty much cried the whole way home from Austin to Lexington. I was hurt, thinking, "I don't even want to come back next year." It still hurts to think about that time.

The following year, which was my senior season, Josh joined

Coach Smith's staff as a graduate assistant. That helped a lot, to be able to get his feedback on my game. I don't think our team reached its full potential that year, but we had some great players like Rajon Rondo and Randolph Morris, who was probably the most gifted big man I'd ever played with.

In terms of knowing the game of basketball, there aren't many coaches better than Tubby Smith, especially when it comes to defense and in-game strategy. There were so many times during my career that we'd be losing at halftime. He'd make some adjustments, and then we'd win the game. Coach Smith also had some unlucky breaks. We often weren't healthy during NCAA Tournament time. If Keith Bogans hadn't sprained his ankle during our victory against Wisconsin in the NCAA Midwest Regional on March 27, 2003, there is no way we would have lost the game against Marquette two days later. We would have won a national championship that year. Any one of my years as a player we could have gone to the Final Four and possibly won it all, but because we didn't, Coach Smith got all the heat and all the pressure. It's hard to get to the Final Four. It's even harder to win a national championship. I think that Coach Smith was underappreciated, but I am thankful for what he taught me. One of these days I'll get into coaching, and I'll be solid because of what I learned from him.

You can't knock the passion of UK fans. They sure care about basketball, but they can be vicious, too. When I was a player they'd get on message boards and start talking trash. My feeling about fans like that was, "You've got to chill out." We were only kids in our late teens and early twenties, but they expected us to be professionals. The fans are so intense because UK is all they have. They can claim the Cincinnati Reds or the Cincinnati Bengals if they want to, but UK represents Kentucky. It's the brand that they identify with the most. They care more about basketball than any other sport.

The fact that I still get recognized by UK fans nowadays is impressive. I was a role player. They always remember my knack for hitting big shots. In fact, during my sophomore year Shagari Alleyne called me "Big Shot Rav." I did my job and thought I played hard, but fans really did respect what I did. That makes me feel good.

30

Patrick Patterson

Prior to signing with UK in 2007, power forward Patrick Patterson won three consecutive state basketball championships at Huntington High School in his hometown of Huntington, West Virginia, and was named a McDonald's All-American his senior season.

During his three-year career at UK Patterson averaged 16.1 points per game and scored 1,564 total points, ranking him thirteenth on the list of the program's all-time leading scorers. He also ranks fourth all-time in field-goal percentage (.5854) and eighth all-time in blocks (152, or an average of 1.6 per game). He is tied with Rick Robey for sixth all-time in double-doubles (30).

Patterson led the 2007–2008 and 2008–2009 squads in rebounding (7.7 per game and 9.3 per game, respectively), and he reached one thousand points in scoring after playing just fifty-eight games. Only nine other UK players reached that milestone in fewer games played.

After being drafted by the NBA's Houston Rockets in 2010, Patterson was traded to the Sacramento Kings in February 2013, then to the Toronto Raptors ten months later.

Patrick Patterson was named SEC Co-Freshman of the Year following the 2007–2008 season. (Courtesy of Victoria Graff.)

What sets the Commonwealth of Kentucky apart from any other place I've been to is how friendly people are. Literally everyone I met during my three years at UK was friendly, open, and welcoming to me. They're a giving people, they don't expect anything back in return, and they're always willing to lend a helping hand. I'm not sure why that is. Maybe it's the way people in Kentucky have always been, or maybe it's the way each person has been brought up.

Former Wildcat player Kenny Walker was an important person to me during my time at UK. I looked up to him. We didn't talk all the time, but he came to practices and to games, and I'd sometimes run into him at the barbershop in Lexington where I'd get my hair cut. He talked to me about his time at Kentucky, what it means to be a Wildcat, and the importance of serving the Lexington community. As a basketball player he taught me how to make myself better. His advice was to enjoy everything that I was doing. "Your time at Kentucky is going to fly by," I remember him telling me. "It's the best time of our life, so embrace it all and don't take anything for granted. Love every single moment of it and overall just have fun. Because if you're not having fun, you shouldn't be doing what you're doing." That was good advice.

During my freshman and sophomore years UK assistant coach Glenn Cyprien was helpful to me both on and off the court. During a game against Ole Miss near the end of my freshman year I started feeling ankle pain, which turned out to be a stress fracture that required season-ending surgery. I was devastated and heartbroken, but Coach Cyprien supported me. He made sure that I was focused and that I wasn't feeling like this injury meant the end of my career. He made sure I was doing my rehab and that I was still attending my college classes—doing all the things I needed to do to get back out there on the court and stay focused on the bigger picture of this injury. He was someone I could lean on if I needed support.

I also appreciate what Coach John Calipari did for me. After he was named the head coach following my sophomore year he told me that he wanted to broaden my game. Right off the bat, whenever we had workouts he put me with the wing players rather than with the "bigs" whom I normally worked out with. He had me working on my angles, my perimeter skills, my jump shot, perimeter defense, footwork, and running the court. It was a tough transition because I had never done that type of work before. During my first two years at UK I had strictly been in the post with my back to the basket, and I rarely took a jump shot. At first I wasn't comfortable with what Coach Calipari was asking me to do, but over time I learned new footwork moves, learned to be more comfortable with my jump shot, learned to space the floor, and developed a part of my game I never knew I was capable of. My father, Buster Patterson, is not from Kentucky, but he encouraged me to adapt to these changes to my game and to embrace them. He told me that these changes would not only make me a better basketball player and prepare me for the future, but they would also make our team better. He was right.

My junior year at Kentucky was my favorite year overall, not only because it was the year I had the most success but also because I enjoyed the relationships I had with my teammates. Coach Calipari is the type of person who loves having players around his family, so we'd often go over to his house to eat, watch TV, or even take naps—just to relax. He likes to build a tightly knit bond with everyone associated with the team. On the court he's strictly our coach. He's focused and in a zone, and he makes you earn everything. Off the court he's just another one of the guys. He's someone you can easily talk to and relate to. I think that's why guys love playing for him.

The support I received from Big Blue Nation still impacts me to this day. It's often said that UK has the best fan base. In my opinion that's a true statement, whether you're talking about college basketball, NBA basketball, or even NFL football. UK fans are everywhere. During my rookie year in the NBA I traveled to China with the Houston Rockets. We visited the Great Wall, and I came across a tourist wearing a Kentucky shirt. He recognized me, and we struck up a conversation right there, halfway around the world from Kentucky. Even in my current home of Sacramento, California, I often encounter Kentucky fans. I'm thankful for that. They're diehard; they care not only about the team as a whole but about each player on the team. They go out of their way to have a conversation with you or to ask to have a picture taken with you. No former UK basketball player I know ever declines such requests, because the fans are so loyal. Fans of Duke University, the University of North Carolina, UCLA, the University of Florida, and University of Michigan basketball are loyal to their teams through and through, but Kentucky fans take loyalty to another level. They're more passionate than any other fans I've met. They care so much about the program, but they hate losing so much that they'll boo their own team If UK is losing to an opponent that they believe the team should beat. That happens in the NBA, but I've never seen that happen in college basketball except at UK.

The fact that I earned my bachelor's degree from UK in three years is going to help me in the future and prepare me for the rest of my life. It sets me apart because there aren't as many players in the NBA who have a college degree. It seems like the current generation of elite players tend to stay one or two years in college and then go to the NBA. This is not surprising because at UK you're always playing in front of packed crowds and against elite competition. That prepares you for the next level in the NBA, playing against the best players in the world, playing in big-time games and having to hit some crunch-time shots. Being at UK, where I embraced that, puts you in the top category and in a more comfortable position when you transition to the NBA.

31

Darius Miller

Maysville, Kentucky, native Darius Miller was named the state's "Mr. Basketball" in 2008 and led Mason County High School to the state championship that year before signing with UK. A four-year letter winner in a one-and-done era, the guard-forward steadily improved each season and finished his career with 1,248 points, which ranks him thirty-fourth on UK's list of all-time leading scorers.

Miller holds the distinction of playing more games for UK than any other player in the program's history (a total of 152), and he is the only UK player to have been named Mr. Basketball in the state, to win a Kentucky boys' state high school basketball championship, and to win an NCAA National Championship.

Between seasons he gained additional basketball experience playing overseas, helping lead Team USA to a gold medal in the U-19 World Championships in New Zealand in the summer of 2009 and representing the United States at the World University Games in China in the summer of 2011.

At the close of the 2011–2012 campaign, which culminated in UK's eighth NCAA National Championship, with a 67–59 victory over Kansas in New Orleans, Miller ranked second on the team in assists

Darius Miller played in 152 games from 2008 to 2012, the most by any Wildcat in the program's history. (Courtesy of Victoria Graff.)

(82, a 2.1-per-game average) and in three-point field goals made (56, a 1.4-per-game average). In the summer of 2012 he was selected by the New Orleans Hornets (now the Pelicans) as the forty-sixth pick in the second round of the NBA draft, joining five of his former UK teammates as draft picks that year.

Being from Kentucky and having the opportunity to play at UK meant a lot to me, especially the support I received from people in my hometown of Maysville after the Chris Lofton ordeal.[1]

My dad, Brian Miller, has been a huge influence on me my whole life, not just limited to the four years I played at UK. He taught me pretty much everything, and he's the reason I started playing basketball in the first place. In fact, the year I was born he was a member of the Morehead State University basketball team, so I learned the game from him. He also taught me how to carry myself and how to treat people. He's been an important role model for me.

Many other people impacted me during my career at UK, including my former teammate Patrick Patterson, who is like a big brother to me. He took me under his wing when I arrived at UK as a freshman. I spent a lot of time with him and saw how he was a leader for our team. Patrick served as a model for me in terms of how to carry myself as a teammate. He led by example.

Josh Harrelson is also like a brother to me. He arrived at UK the same time I did (2008), so we were close from the very beginning. To this day I'm still close with most of my former UK teammates.

When I was a young boy Tony Delk was one of my favorite players. I wouldn't say that I modeled my game after his, but I enjoyed watching how he played. He played really hard, was a good scorer and an entertaining player to watch. So it meant a lot to me when he joined Coach John Calipari's coaching staff as an assistant. He was very helpful and taught me a lot of things on and off the court.

Assistant Coach Kenny Payne also did a lot for me. He made me work hard. I think that helped me to become a better player. He taught me a lot about the game of basketball, especially what's expected at the professional level, because of his experience.[2] I hung around him a lot.

The Big Blue Nation fan base really impacted me. In my opinion they're some of the best fans in the world. They do a great job supporting the team with events like the Big Blue Madness campout every fall. Me being a hometown kid, they showed me a lot of support throughout my four years, but especially during my freshman year, when our team was struggling a bit. Every tournament game we played in a neutral setting felt like home-court advantage because of how many UK fans would show up. Even some of our away games felt like home games because there were so many Kentucky fans there.

Coach Cal's first year at UK was a completely different situation than the one I was in my freshman year. We had a really successful team that year. I learned a new system, and it was a lot of fun. Of course, winning the 2012 national championship in New Orleans my senior year was a blessing. We had put in a lot of hard work up to that point, but to finally achieve our goal was amazing. The chemistry on our championship team was unique. Nobody cared who got the credit. It was all about us winning and having fun. That's what we did. We were just out there trying to have fun and enjoy the moments that we have. It was good for all of us. No one had a huge ego.

In May 2012 our team was invited to the White House to be congratulated for our championship win by President Barack Obama. I presented him with a number-one UK jersey. It was an incredible experience to walk in to the White House and to visit the president. I was honored to be a part of it all, and I'll never forget.

32

John Wall

A key member of Coach John Calipari's first recruiting UK class, John Wall averaged 22.1 points, 5.2 rebounds, and 2.0 steals per game as a senior at Word of God Christian Academy in his hometown of Raleigh, North Carolina. In 2009 he was ranked the number-one high school prospect by Rivals.com and was named a McDonald's All-American.

At UK, Wall dished out 241 assists during his freshman year, which broke the UK single-season record of 232, set by Roger Harden in 1986. Wall also set the single-game record in assists, with sixteen, in a victory against Hartford, which broke a single-game record of fifteen set by Travis Ford in 1993. He led the 2009–2010 Wildcats in steals (an average of 1.8 per game), assists (an average of 6.5 per game), and scoring (an average of 16.6 per game).

Wall closed out his UK career by being named the 2010 Adolph Rupp Trophy National Player of the Year, the Yahoo Sports National Player of the Year, and the Rivals.com National Player of the Year. In June 2010 Wall became the first player in UK history to be named a number-one NBA pick when he was chosen by the Washington Wizards. He lives in suburban Maryland.

Prior to signing with UK in 2009, John Wall was a finalist for the Naismith National High School Player of the Year. (Courtesy of Victoria Graff.)

My mom, Frances Pulley, has always played an important role in my life. After my dad passed away when I was nine years old, she worked three or four jobs to make ends meet and to make sure that my sisters and I had a good life. She provided us with opportunities to reach our goals. There were times when Mom didn't pay an electric bill so that I could compete in an Amateur Athletic Union basketball tournament. She's been one of the biggest influential figures in my life.

Kentucky is a special place to be and a special place to play basketball. The Wildcat fans are amazing, twenty-four thousand strong at all the home games. What sets the state apart from others is that the people there love basketball so much. There are no NBA teams, NFL teams, or Major League Baseball teams in the state, so there's nothing bigger than UK basketball from a sports standpoint.

I had always liked UK, and I made a couple of recruiting visits to the campus when I was in high school. I was impressed by the fans and how they treated me as a recruit, but the biggest reason I signed with UK had to do with Coach John Calipari being hired as the head basketball coach. My goal was to be in a program where I felt comfortable and was able to have fun. When I first met Coach Cal he seemed more interested in me as a person than as a player. We spent most of our time talking about life, not basketball. That impressed me, because when you're being recruited you don't want to hear a coach beg you to death and talk to you only about basketball, because there's more to life. Choosing the college program you want to play for is a big decision, and once you sign the letter of intent, you've given your commitment. Coach Cal made the decision to sign with UK easy for me. My mom trusted him right away, and he became a father figure to me.

Even though playing in the NBA was a lifelong dream of mine, I did not sign with UK knowing I'd stay just stay one year and then head to the NBA, but that's how it was perceived by some people. After our team lost to West Virginia University in the 2010 NCAA Tournament, a lot of us wanted to return the next season. I signed with UK to play basketball and try to help the program win a national championship. That was my goal. But after our 2009–2010 season I had a rare opportunity to be the number-one NBA draft pick that year, so that's what I decided to do. I wanted to reach my dream of being an NBA player, but at the same time I did sit back and think, "I wish I could play at UK again." But you've got to do what you've got to do. I do plan to return to UK to get my degree.

The people who were most influential to me during my year at UK were the basketball coaching staff, my teammates, and Randall Cobb,[1] who played on the UK football team. I looked up to Randall as a star on the football field and for how he played multiple positions. He was real competitive and a class-act guy. I watched every game I could to see how he performed. Every time he touched the ball he was trying to make a fundamental play, not a heroic play. That impressed me.

My coaches at UK taught me ways to become a better leader not only to lead the team but to go out on the basketball court, have fun, and enjoy myself. I could talk to them about anything. If I was having a bad day or if I was down about something, they'd pick me up. They didn't babysit me and my teammates, but they wanted to make sure we were doing the right things on and off the court. I related to Rod Strickland[2] in particular because he was a point guard during his college and NBA career. He taught me some moves and ways I could improve my game. In my book he was one of the best NBA point guards of his era, so it wasn't hard for me to learn from a guy like that.

Another person influential to me was Reese Kemp,[3] a boy from Nicholasville, Kentucky, who has cystic fibrosis and diabetes. I had the opportunity to meet Reese at Kentucky Children's Hospital in 2009, and he's been in my life ever since. He's attended some Washington Wizards home games, and today I'm kind of like a big brother to him.

Playing my first few games as a Wildcat was special to me, especially having the game-winning shot against Miami University during a home game on November 16, 2009. That was my first game as a Wildcat. Other highlights for me were hitting a big-time layup during our win against the UConn Huskies in the SEC/Big East Challenge at Madison Square Garden and traveling to Cancun, Mexico, where we won the Cancun Challenge against Stanford University. Beating the University of North Carolina at Rupp Arena was also memorable, since I'm from that state. And being part of the team that won UK its two thousandth game against Drexel University on December 21, 2009, was big-time special. We also had fun during our run in the 2010 NCAA Tournament.

As for the Big Blue Nation fans, they believed in me and what I could do on the basketball court. As a person and as a player I tried to be a class act. I think they understood that. They welcomed me with open arms, and I'm always welcomed back in Lexington. It's like a second home to me. It's amazing how supportive the fans were, wanting to talk to me after classes and sitting outside Wildcat Lodge most every day waiting to get an autograph or to meet me. It was exciting. Some days I'd want a break from it, but I'd also keep in mind that I had a once-in-a-lifetime opportunity at UK.

When I was given an opportunity to become the starting point guard for the Washington Wizards, I knew what would be expected of me thanks to the leadership lessons I learned at UK. That certainly helped me in my current role. I'm grateful that fans of the Big Blue Nation support me because I sure support them. Whenever I have the opportunity to see a game in Rupp Arena I travel back for that. I no longer wear a Kentucky uniform, but in September 2013

I returned to Rupp Arena with the Washington Wizards to compete against former Wildcats Anthony Davis and Darius Miller and the rest of the New Orleans Pelicans in an NBA preseason game. To be able to play on that court again was big-time special.

Acknowledgments

I'm indebted to many terrific people who helped me believe in this book and encouraged me to see it through to completion. First, thanks to University Press of Kentucky acquisitions editor Ashley Runyon for her steadfast support of this project and for encouraging me to stay the course when the manuscript was in its early stages.

When I began to invite former UK basketball players and coaches to be interviewed for *Wildcat Memories*, I wondered: Would they open up to a nonsportswriter about the people who impacted them during their time representing UK? The majority agreed to lend their "voice," and I am thankful for their willingness to do so. This book would not have been possible without their cooperation. Special thanks to Ed Beck, the first person I interviewed. His replies to my questions were so rich with detail that it validated what I set out to accomplish in this book. Dan Issel, UK's all-time leading scorer and the second person I interviewed, provided more validation with his perspective and his affinity for the UK basketball program. I'm appreciative—and honored—that he agreed to write the foreword for *Wildcat Memories*.

Behind the scenes, numerous people facilitated interviews with some of the sources in this book, including Calvin Andrews, Mary Lee Draper, Scott Hall, John Hayden, Trenten Hilburn, Daren Jenkins, Susan Johnson, Caitlin Mahoney, Odell McCants,

Deb Moore, Patrick Rees, Jon Schulman, and Brian Travis. Others helped me secure photos and other important material, including Ed and Faye Beck, Darrell Bird, Janie Daugherty, Eddie and Pat Ford, Ron Garrison, Victoria Graff, Laura Nicholson, Susan Nicholson, Mike Pratt, Elizabeth Whitt, and the staff at the University of Kentucky Special Collections Library and the University of Kentucky Digital Library Services. Thanks also to Carol Sickman-Garner for her assistance in editing this book.

Thanks as well to my brother, Bob, and to the many members of the far-flung Brunk and Dick clans who supported my efforts. I'm also grateful to my mother-in-law, Barbara Goran, for cheering me on. Friends and colleagues who provided important encouragement to me along the way include Dale Austin, Jordan Bleyle, Dean and Ruth Cook, Kevin Cook, Dave Good, Kerrell Farmelant, Matt Farmelant, Scott Farmelant, Denise Fulton, Debra Isaacs, Rick and Lisa Lofgren, John McHugh, Dean and Marcia Nelson, Anita Palmer, Wayne and Alice Rogers, Jo Ann Rudolph, Scott Rudolph, Sterz, Colleen Rush, Guy Smith, Dave Weiner, and Sandra Millers Younger.

My mom and dad, Bill and Genevieve Brunk, deserve special thanks. They moved our family from North Chili, New York, to Wilmore, Kentucky, in the summer of 1973, when I was seven years old. This exposed me and my brother to the friendly people and magical landscape of Central Kentucky. Mom taught me the importance of being a good listener, and Dad supported my enthusiasm for basketball from the get-go. In fact, he hired a concrete worker to pour a square slab in the back of our house and hired another man to construct and position a metal pole to hold a basketball goal and rim. There, with horses on one side of our property and cows on another, I spent hours imitating (poorly) the moves of certain UK players, often to the steady chirping of crickets in the background.

My wife, Vickie, also deserves recognition. Early on in this project she helped me work through a period of self-doubt—an affliction every writer I know wrestles with from time to time. Before I spent too much time second-guessing my efforts, Vickie offered a challenge. "Why not you?" she asked matter-of-factly. Those three words were a game changer.

Finally, thanks to all of the people I encountered as a young boy growing up in the Commonwealth of Kentucky and to all of the Wildcat teams and coaches I've followed through the years. My blood runs blue because of you.

Author's Note

Although each new campaign adds to the Wildcats' rich history, the historical material included in this book does not extend beyond the 2012–2013 season, due to the demands of publishing. The narratives contained in *Wildcat Memories* are based on interviews I conducted with thirty-one UK men's basketball players and coaches between March 2012 and September 2013. I sought input from standout players and coaches who represented the basketball program in each decade dating back to the 1940s in order to create a linear timeline for the reader. The majority of interviews were conducted by telephone, but some were conducted in person. I asked each source the same general set of questions and added others based on that person's unique contributions to the program.

The interviewees responded to questions based on their memories of the past, as filtered by their position and perspective in the present. My role was to mold the full interviews into a coherent first-person narrative that reflected each interviewee's unique "voice." This involved enhancing readability, coherence, and narrative flow. I added transitional words to connect or clarify passages of text, and I eliminated verbal space fillers—"ums," "uhs," and the like. I cut repetitive passages, digressions, and material that was out of context or unclear. After I shaped each narrative, I provided each source the opportunity to review it for factual accuracy as a courtesy. Based on their feedback I made changes or edits as needed. Once completed, each narrative became its own chapter, and I organized the chapters in historical order.

Notes

Introduction

1. © University of Kentucky, all rights reserved, University of Kentucky Athletics: William B. Keightley Oral History Project, Louie B. Nunn Center for Oral History, University of Kentucky Libraries.

2. © University of Kentucky, all rights reserved, University of Kentucky Athletics: Adolph Rupp Oral History Project, Louie B. Nunn Center for Oral History, University of Kentucky Libraries.

3. © University of Kentucky, all rights reserved, University of Kentucky Athletics: Adolph Rupp Oral History Project, Louie B. Nunn Center for Oral History, University of Kentucky Libraries.

1. Basil Hayden

1. Brent Kelley, "Basil Hayden: Kentucky's First Basketball All-American," *Sports Collectors Digest,* Feb. 11, 1994, 100–101.

2. US Route 25 stretches between Covington, Kentucky, and Brunswick, Georgia.

6. Ed Beck

1. Albert Benjamin ("Happy") Chandler was Kentucky's governor for two terms: from 1935 to 1939 and from 1955 to 1959.

2. Frank Graves Dickey served as UK's president from 1956 to 1963.

10. Dan Issel

1. This passage is contained in Theodore Roosevelt's "Citizenship in a Republic" speech, delivered on Apr. 23, 1910, in Paris, France. The speech is also known as "The Man in the Arena."

2. Armand Angelucci went on to become a district judge in Fayette County, Kentucky.

11. Joe B. Hall

1. Former Bethel College men's basketball coach Lon Varnell joined Adolph Rupp's staff at UK in 1944 and left four years later to coach at the University of the South.

2. Henry ("Hank") Iba was the head men's basketball coach at Oklahoma State University for thirty-six seasons, retiring in 1970. He coached US Olympic men's basketball teams in 1964, 1968, and 1972.

13. Kevin Grevey

1. Jim Duff is currently president and CEO of the Newseum in Washington, DC.

14. Jack ("Goose") Givens

1. Givens graced the Apr. 3, 1978, cover of *Sports Illustrated* following UK's win over Duke University in the NCAA National Championship that year. The headline read "The Goose Was Golden."

16. Kyle Macy

1. Bob Bradley is UK's associate athletics director for student services. He has worked at the university since 1977.

18. Jim Master

1. Donald Webb passed away on July 19, 2013, at the age of seventy-four.

19. Roger Harden

1. Chuck Melcher and Charlotte Melcher, PhD, are counselors in Lexington.

20. Deron Feldhaus

1. Allen Feldhaus Sr. played at UK from 1960 to 1962.

2. Allen Feldhaus Jr. is the head basketball coach at Madison Central High School in Richmond, Kentucky.

3. Willie Feldhaus is the head basketball coach at Russell County High School in Russell Springs, Kentucky.

21. Travis Ford

1. Each year Eddie Ford directs Kentucky HoopFest, a two-hundred-plus-team event in Louisville that features summer travel teams from across North America.

24. Allen Edwards

1. Father J. Edward Bradley was pastor of Holy Name of Jesus Catholic Church in Henderson, Kentucky, from 1995 to 2011.

26. Orlando ("Tubby") Smith

1. C. M. Newton, who played guard for UK from 1949 to 1951, was instrumental in hiring Smith's predecessor, Rick Pitino, as head coach. He was inducted into the Naismith Memorial Basketball Hall of Fame in 2000.

2. George Felton served as an assistant coach to Tubby Smith at UK during the 1997–1998 campaign.

3. In 1988, Will Perdue was named the Southeastern Conference Player of the Year and the SEC Male Athlete of the Year.

4. Stu Jackson was executive vice president of basketball operations for the National Basketball Association from 2007 to 2013.

31. Darius Miller

1. Chris Lofton, another standout from Mason County High School, was not offered a scholarship from UK in 2004, so he signed with the University of Tennessee, where he became a star player.

2. A four-year letter winner at Louisville, Payne was selected nineteenth in the first round of the 1989 NBA draft and played four years for the Philadelphia 76ers.

32. John Wall

1. Randall Cobb was drafted by the Green Bay Packers in the second round of the 2011 NFL draft.

2. Rod Strickland was a member of John Calipari's coaching staff from 2009 through the 2013–2014 campaign.

3. Reese Kemp is the founder of Reese's Resources, Inc., a foundation aimed at raising awareness of cystic fibrosis.

Index

ABA. *See* American Basketball Association (ABA)
ABA Championships, 1975, 73
Adolph Rupp Trophy National Player of the Year, 217
African Americans, 25, 30, 70–71, 127
Ainge, Danny, 65
Akins, C. B., Sr., 172
Akron Goodyear Wingfoots, 55
All-American honors, 89, 96, 123, 140, 167; Johnny Cox and, 55, 56; Cliff Hagan and, 33, 34; Basil Hayden and, 9, 13, 16, 17; Wallace "Wah Wah" Jones and, 20; Kyle Macy and, 115, 116; Frank Ramsey and, 41, 45
Allen, Forrest C. "Phog," 4, 6, 53, 60
Allen Fieldhouse, 60
Alleyne, Shagari, 206
Alumni Gym, 7, 10, 23, 28, 35–36
Amateur Athletic Union (AAU), 127
American Basketball Association (ABA), xi, 41, 55, 61, 73, 76, 79–80, 89

Anderson, Derek, 175–80, 203
Anderson, Derek, Jr., 177
Angelucci, Armand "Mondo," 2, 5, 77–78, 229n2 (chap. 10)
Angelucci, Joyce, 2, 5, 77–78
Appel, Max, 164–65
Armstrong, Army, 37
Asbury Theological Seminary, 47
Ashland High School, 67
Ashland Oil Radio Network, 35
assists, 67, 89, 115, 137, 138, 149, 213, 215, 217
Atlanta Braves, 22
Atlanta Hawks, 103, 108, 161
Auburn University, 90
Auerbach, Red, 42

Badgett, Thomas "Brown," Sr., 133
Ball, Alva, 21
Barker, Cliff, 9
Baylor University, 9
Beal, Dicky, 131
Beard, Ralph, 9, 27
Bearup, Bret, 131
Beck, Billie, 2, 50, 51, 52, 53
Beck, Ed, 2, 3, 47–54

Beck, Faye, 47, 49, 54
Beck, Jonathan Edward, 49, 54
Bellarmine University, 76
Bennett, Winston, 158, 178
Big Blue Nation. *See* Wildcat fans
Birdsong, Otis, 112
Blanda, George, 21
blocks, 187, 194, 195, 207
Blue Grass Tours, 19
Bogans, Keith, 203, 205
Boston Braves, 22
Boston Celtics, 33, 41, 42, 109,
    112, 130, 183
Boston University, 130
Boswell, Bill, 83–84
Bowie, Sam, 117, 132
Box, Larkie, 2, 83
Bradley, Bob, 120, 230n1 (chap.
    16)
Bradley, Ed, 172, 231n1 (chap. 24)
Brajuha, Mandy. *See* Polley,
    Mandy
Breeding, Sheila, 172–73
Broadbent, Dick, 126
"Broncomania," 78
Brooks, Delray, 178
Bryan Station High School
    (Lexington), 103, 105, 108
Bryant, Paul "Bear," 20, 21–22
Buchheit, George C., 14
Butler University, 166

Calipari, John, 167, 187, 190,
    215, 231n2 (chap. 32); hiring
    of, 193–94, 209–10; NCAA
    Championships and, 86, 216;
    John Wall and, 217, 219

Campbellsville University, 149, 151
Campus Crusade for Christ, xii,
    139
Cancun Challenge, 221
Candler School of Theology, 47
Carrier, Josh, 197–98, 204–5
Casey, Mike, 79, 91
Caywood, Orel, 44
Central Missouri State University,
    81, 85
Centre College, 76
Chandler, Albert Benjamin
    "Happy," 2, 43, 51–52, 53, 64,
    229n1 (chap. 6)
Chandler, Joseph, 43
Chapman, Rex, 129
Charlotte Hornets, 89, 93
Chicago Bears, 135
Chicago Bulls, 115
Chicago White Sox, 61
Chicago Zephyrs, 55
China, 211, 213
Claiborne, Jerry, 30
Claiborne Farm, 4, 111–12,
    133–34
Clark County High School, 16
Clemson University, 31
Cleveland Cavaliers, 123, 175
Cleveland Pipers, 55
Cliff Hagan Boys and Girls Club,
    36–37
coal industry, 49, 133
Cobb, Randall, 220, 231n1 (chap.
    32)
Colorado, 78
Commonwealth Stadium, 27, 31
Conley, Gene, 65

Conley, Larry, 67–71
Connors, Kevin Joseph "Chuck,"
    65
Continental Basketball
    Association, 169
Converse, 67
Cox, Bill, 57
Cox, Johnny, 55–58
Cox, Lula Mae, 57
Creighton University, 129
Crum, Denny, 83
Cuba High School, 151
Curry, Bill, 30–31
Cynthiana High School, 83–84
Cyprien, Glenn, 209

Dampier, Louis, 59, 95
Daugherty, Janie, 13
Davis, Anthony, 194, 222
Davis, Johnny, 112
"Death Penalty," 38
Delk, Tony, 169, 171, 178, 215
Denver Broncos, 78
Denver Nuggets, xi, 73, 78
Derek Anderson Foundation, 177
Dickey, Frank Graves, 51, 52–53,
    229n2 (chap. 6)
Ditka, Mike, 135
Donovan, Billy, 146, 152, 158, 159,
    171
Doss High School (Louisville), 175
double-doubles, 61, 89, 207
Drennon, Herb, 70
Drexel University, 194, 221
Duff, Jim, 101, 230n1 (chap. 13)
Duke University, 47, 84, 86,
    130, 166, 211; 1978 NCAA

Championship and, 60, 103,
    104, 109, 115, 230n1 (chap. 14)

Eastern Kentucky University, 57,
    145, 151
Edwards, Allen, 169–74
Edwards, Doug, 170
Edwards, Laura Mae, 172
Edwards, Steve, 170
Eklund, Ray, 13
Ellis, Ray, 44
Epps, Anthony, 149, 203
ESPN, 35, 37, 67
Estill, Marquis, 187–91
Europe, 160
Evans, Billy, 46

"Fabulous Five," 3, 9–10, 19, 36
Farmer, Richie, 143, 148
Farris, Patricia, 189
Farris, Ronetta, 190
Faulconer, Barbara, 171–72
Faulconer, Ted, 171–72
Feldhaus, Allen, Jr., 146, 230n2
    (chap. 20)
Feldhaus, Allen, Sr., 143, 144, 145,
    146, 230n1 (chap. 20)
Feldhaus, Deron, 143–48
Feldhaus, Willie, 145, 146, 230n3
    (chap. 20)
Fellowship of Christian Athletes,
    165
Felton, George, 183, 231n2 (chap.
    26)
"Fiddlin' Five," 11, 47
Fitch, Gerald, 203
Fleming Neon High School, 57

Florida State University, 170
Ford, Eddie, 151, 230n1 (chap. 21)
Ford, Pat, 151
Ford, Travis, 131, 149–54, 217
Fort Knox, 44
Fox Sports Network, 67
France, 10
Freedom Hall, 91, 120, 125
free throws, 7, 73, 95, 109, 115,
    123, 131, 137, 149, 195
Fritz, Jane, 164
Fritz, Robert, 164
Fugitive, The (TV show), 78

Gant, Bill, 37
Gates, Bill, 180
Gentry, Tom, 80
Georgia, 161
Georgia Tech, 10, 44
Gillispie, Billy, 163, 193
Givens, Betty, 107
Givens, Jack "Goose," 2, 7, 60,
    103–8, 230n1 (chap. 14)
Glory Road (2006), 59
Great Depression, 16
Greater Liberty Baptist Church,
    2, 105
Grevey, Kevin, 3, 5, 95–102
Grevey Foundation, 95
Groat, Dick, 65
Groza, Alex, 9

Hagan, Cliff, xi, 3, 10, 33–39, 45
Hagan, Martha, 35, 37
Hall, Charles C. "Bill," 84
Hall, Joe B., 81–88, 133; as
    assistant coach, 76, 81, 85; as

coach, 3, 5, 82, 86–88, 184;
    Larry Conley and, 69–70; Jack
    "Goose" Givens and, 105–6;
    Kevin Grevey and, 97–100,
    101; Roger Harden and, 139,
    140, 142; Derrick Hord and,
    127; Kyle Macy and, 117–19,
    120; as player, 2, 81, 84–85;
    retirement of, 129; Rick Robey
    and, 111; Rupp and, 76, 81,
    84–85, 87–88; succeeding
    Rupp, 60, 81, 85
Hall, Katharine, 81, 85–86,
    119–20
Hancock, Arthur B., 111
Hancock, Seth W., 4, 111–12,
    133–34
Hancock, Walker, 112
Harden, Al, 140
Harden, Joseph, 137, 139–40, 141
Harden, Myrna, 140
Harden, Roger, xii, 137–42, 217
Harlan High School, 21
Harrelson, Josh, 215
Harris, Marshall, 126
Haskins, Don, 71
Hatton, Vernon, 11, 48
Hayden, Annie Brown, 15
Hayden, Basil, 9, 13–17
Hayden, Ellis, 16
Hayden, Joseph Wallace, 15
Hayden, Leo, 15
Hayes, Chuck, 195–99, 204
Hayes, Elvin, 95
Hazard Christmas Parade, 134
Hazard High School, 55, 57
Hobbs, Dave, 203–4

Hord, Derrick, 123–28
horse industry, 23, 49, 63, 65–66, 80, 111–12, 126, 133–34
Houston Rockets, 195, 207, 211
Huntington High School (W.Va.), 207

Iba, Hank, 84, 230n2 (chap. 11)
Indiana, 134, 137, 139
Indiana Basketball Hall of Fame, 115, 117
Indiana Pacers, 109, 115, 159
Indianapolis Olympians, 19
Indiana University, 7, 36, 166
injuries, 156, 179–80, 189–90, 194, 205, 209
International Basketball Association, 169
Issel, Dan, xi–xii, 2, 5, 41, 59–60, 73–80, 95, 113, 129, 164
Italy, 161
Ivey, Don, 70

Jackson, Stu, 183, 231n4 (chap. 26)
Jackson, V. A., 100–101
Japan, 123, 143, 147
jersey retirement, 17, 19, 58, 143, 148
Jim Phelan Coach of the Year Award, 181
"Joe B. and Denny Show, The" (radio show), 83
Johnson, Spencer, 158
Jones, Edna, 19, 21
Jones, Hugh, 22
Jones, Wallace "Wah Wah," 9, 19–23

Jordan, Michael, 131
J. Walter Kennedy Citizenship Award, 73

Kansas State University, 10, 33, 41
Keeneland, xii, 23, 80
Keightley, William "Bill," 1, 106–7, 112, 120, 126, 147, 159, 163–64, 183–84
Kelley, Brent, 14
Kemp, Reese, 220–21, 231n3 (chap. 32)
Kenton Station Golf Course, 143
Kentucky Athletic Hall of Fame, 112
Kentucky Basketball Academy, 155, 160
Kentucky Colonels, xi, 41, 61, 73, 76, 78, 80, 89, 92, 94
Kentucky High School Athletic Association, 127
Kentucky High School Basketball All-Star, 175
Kentucky High School Basketball Championships, 21, 67, 91, 145, 213; 1949, 33, 36, 37; 1955, 55, 57
Kentucky High School Basketball Hall of Fame, 19
Kentucky High School Basketball Tournament, xi
Kentucky Wesleyan College, 16
Kentucky Wildcats. See UK basketball
Kindy, David, 189–90
King, Helen, 50
Kron, Tom, 70

Laettner, Christian, 130, 148
Lancaster, Harry, 28, 45, 46, 50, 51, 53, 58, 63, 69
Ledford, Cawood, 7, 69, 125, 135
Lee, Albert B., 2, 105–6
Lee, James, 105–6, 145
Lofton, Chris, 215, 231n1 (chap. 31)
Los Angeles Lakers, 61, 137, 140
Louisiana State University, 10
Loyola University Maryland, 181

Macauley, Ed, 33
Macy, Bob, 117
Macy, Kyle, 6–7, 115–21
Macy, Tina, 117
Madison Central High School, 187, 230n2 (chap. 20)
Madisonville High School, 44
Madisonville-North Hopkins High School, 151
Major League Baseball (MLB), 22, 61, 64, 65, 219
Majors, Johnny, 135
Maker's Mark, xii
Maravich, "Pistol Pete," 93
Marquette University, 205
Martinez, Gimel, 171
Mashburn, Jamal, 130, 152–53
Mason County High School, 143, 145, 213, 231n1 (chap. 31)
Master, Jim, 131–35
Mattox, Bernadette, 25
Maysville, 143, 145, 213, 215
McCarty, Walter, 171
McDonald's All-Americans, 123, 131, 137, 207, 217

McGinnis, "Big Mac" Laurence, 37
McIntosh High School (Peachtree City, Ga.), 161
McMackin, Marta, 126, 184
Mears, Ray, 93
Meeks, Jodie, 73, 115
Melcher, Charlotte, 139, 230n1 (chap. 19)
Melcher, Chuck, xii, 139, 230n1 (chap. 19)
Memorial Coliseum, 2, 7, 38, 54, 63; high school games and, 57, 171; opening of, 10, 28, 29; practices and, 5, 45, 119, 178; replacing of, 60; Wildcat fans and, 79, 91, 93
Mercer, Ron, 159, 178
Miami Heat, 175
Miami Hurricanes, 170
Miami Senior High School (Fla.), 169, 171
Miami University, 221
Michigan State University, 204
Middleton, George, 127
Miller, Brian, 215
Miller, Darius, 213–16, 222
Mills, Cameron, 173
Minnesota Timberwolves, 197
Minnesota Twins, 61
Mississippi State University, 59, 79, 99
Modesto Christian High School (Calif.), 195
Mohammed, Nazr, 171, 190
Morehead State University, 35, 57, 115, 118, 145, 169, 215

Morris, Randolph, 205
Moss, Ravi, 197–98, 201–6
"Mr. Basketball," 139; Derek
    Anderson, 175; Johnny Cox,
    55; Jack "Goose" Givens, 103;
    Roger Harden, 137; Chuck
    Hayes, 195; Kyle Macy, 115;
    Jim Master, 131; Darius Miller,
    213; Jared Prickett, 155
"Mr. Wildcat." See Keightley,
    William "Bill"
Mullin, Chris, 131
Mumme, Hal, 31
Murray State University, 35, 94,
    151
Music City Bowl, 31
"My Old Kentucky Home," 100

Naismith, James, 6, 39
Naismith College Coach of the
    Year, 181
Naismith Memorial Basketball
    Hall of Fame, 27, 35, 41, 73,
    231n1 (chap. 26)
Naismith National High School
    Player of the Year, 218
Nash, Charles "Cotton," 2, 59,
    61–66, 95
Nash, Julie, 61, 65–66
National Basketball Association
    (NBA), 46, 75, 99, 118, 131,
    165–66, 170, 219, 231n4;
    Atlanta Hawks, 103, 108, 161;
    Boston Celtics, 33, 41, 42,
    109, 112, 140, 183; Charlotte
    Hornets, 89, 93; Chicago
    Bulls, 115; Chicago Zephyrs,
    55; Cleveland Cavaliers, 123,
    175; college degrees and, 211;
    Denver Nuggets, xi, 73, 78;
    drafted from UK and, 33, 41,
    82, 109, 111, 123, 137, 140;
    drafted from UK in 1990s and
    2000s and, 175, 194, 207, 215,
    217, 220; Houston Rockets,
    195, 207, 211; Indiana Pacers,
    109, 115, 159; Indianapolis
    Olympians, 19; Los Angeles
    Lakers, 61, 137, 140; Major
    League Baseball (MLB) and,
    65; Miami Heat, 175; New
    Orleans Hornets, 215; New
    Orleans Pelicans, 215, 222;
    Orlando Magic, 103; Phoenix
    Suns, 109, 115; preseason
    game at Rupp Arena and, 222;
    Sacramento Kings, 195, 197,
    207; San Francisco Warriors,
    61; St. Louis Hawks, 33;
    Toronto Raptors, 195, 207;
    UK basketball and, 5, 79–80,
    82, 194, 215, 217; Washington
    Bullets, 95, 101; Washington
    Wizards, 217, 221, 222;
    Wildcat fans and, 108, 113,
    121
National Collegiate Athletic
    Association (NCAA)
    Championships. See NCAA
    Championships
National Collegiate Athletic
    Association (NCAA)
    Tournament. See NCAA
    Tournament

National Collegiate Basketball
Hall of Fame, 81
National Football League (NFL),
78, 219, 231n1 (chap. 32)
National Industrial Basketball
League, 55
National Invitational Tournament
(NIT), 194
National Invitational Tournament
(NIT) Championships, 9, 35
National Invitational Tournament
(NIT) Selection Committee,
27
NBA. See National Basketball
Association (NBA)
NBA Championships, xi, 36, 41;
1958, 33; 1978, 95; 1981, 109;
2006, 175
NCAA basketball scholarships,
103
NCAA Championships, xi, 182,
205; 1940s, 9, 35; 1948, 3, 9,
19; 1949, 10; 1951, 10, 27, 33,
41; 1958, 11, 47, 48, 51, 54, 55;
1966, 59, 67, 68, 69, 70–71,
92; 1975, 95; 1978, 60, 81, 103,
104, 109, 115, 118, 145, 230n1
(chap. 14); 1996, 130, 155, 159,
161, 165, 169, 175, 178; 1997,
130; 1998, 130, 161, 169, 173,
181; 2006, 159; 2007, 159;
2012, 194, 213, 216; football,
135; Adolph Rupp and, 6, 48,
62, 86, 135; UK basketball
and, 7, 11, 36, 44, 60, 86–87,
94, 184, 213
NCAA Football Hall of Fame, 135

NCAA Infractions Committee, 38
NCAA: practice rules and, 146–
47; UK basketball three years'
probation and, 25, 28, 129–30,
143
NCAA Tournament, 10–11, 36,
60, 102, 166, 193, 205; 2009–
2010 season, 220, 221; Elite
Eight and, 194, 202, 204; Final
Four Most Outstanding Player,
103, 161; Final Fours, 39, 154,
194; Most Outstanding Player,
194; Regional Finals, 94, 129,
130, 148; Sweet Sixteens, 181,
182
New Orleans Hornets, 215
New Orleans Pelicans, 215, 222
Newton, Charles Martin "C. M.,"
25–31, 45, 133, 143, 183,
231n1 (chap. 26)
New York Knicks, 29–30
New Zealand, 213
Nike, 103
Noel, Nerlens, 179–80, 194
Nutter Field House, 31
Nutter Training Center, 31

Obama, Barack, 216
O'Brien, John, 158
Ohio State University, 94, 175, 179
Oklahoma A&M, 10
Oklahoma State University, 149,
230n2 (chap. 11)
Olympics, 27, 230n2 (chap. 11);
1948, 9–10, 19
Orlando Comets, 103
Orlando Magic, 103

Outback Bowl, 31
Owensboro High School, 33, 36, 37

Padgett, Scott, 171
Pan American Games: 1975, 110, 112; 1983, 131
Parish, Robert, 112
Paris High School, 13, 15
Parson, Don, 151
Parsons, Dick, 98, 118–19
Patterson, Buster, 210
Patterson, Patrick, 3, 193, 207–11, 215
Payne, Kenny, 216, 231n2 (chap. 31)
Peach Bowl, 31
Pelphrey, John, 143, 148, 152
Penn State University, 31
Perdue, Will, 183, 231n3 (chap. 26)
Perkins, Sam, 131
Peru High School (Ind.), 117
Phoenix Suns, 109, 115
Pitino, Rick, 203; Derek Anderson and, 178; Allen Edwards and, 169, 171, 173; Deron Feldhaus and, 146, 147, 148; Travis Ford and, 150, 152, 153; hiring of, 29–30, 130, 231n1 (chap. 26); NCAA Championships and, 86; Jared Prickett and, 158, 159; Jeff Sheppard and, 161, 164, 165, 166, 167; Orlando "Tubby" Smith and, 181, 183, 184
point-scoring: Derek Anderson

and, 175; Johnny Cox and, 55; Marquis Estill and, 187; Deron Feldhaus and, 143; field-goal percentage and, 109, 124, 143, 149, 175, 187, 188, 207; Travis Ford and, 149; Jack "Goose" Givens and, 7, 103; Kevin Grevey and, 95; Cliff Hagan and, 10, 33, 34, 36; Roger Harden and, 137; Vernon Hatton and, 11; Basil Hayden and, 13; Chuck Hayes and, 195; Derrick Hord and, 123, 124; Dan Issel and, 5, 59–60, 73, 74, 77, 95, 129; Wallace "Wah Wah" Jones and, 19, 21; Kyle Macy and, 115; Jamal Mashburn and, 130; Jim Master and, 131; Darius Miller and, 213, 215; Ravi Moss and, 201; Charles "Cotton" Nash and, 61, 95; Patrick Patterson and, 207; Mike Pratt and, 89, 90; Frank Ramsey and, 10, 41; Rick Robey and, 109; Jeff Sheppard and, 161, 162; Junior Kenny "Sky" Walker and, 129; John Wall and, 217
point-shaving scandal, 10
Polley, Mandy, 198
Pope, Mark, 171
Potter, Cliffordean, 37
Potter, Hugh, Jr., 37
Potter, Hugh, Sr., 37
Pratt, Mike, 76, 77, 79, 89–94
Precious Present, The (Johnson), 158

Price, Mark, 131
Prickett, Jared, 155–60
Providence College, 130, 146, 152, 183
Pulley, Frances, 219
Purdue University, 115, 117

Qualls, Kent, 125
Qualls, Kevin, 125
Qualls, Larry, 125

radio, 21, 35, 37, 44; Joe B. Hall and, 81, 83; Cawood Ledford and, 7, 69, 125, 135; UK Radio Network, 89, 92
Ramsey, Frank, 10, 36, 41–46
Ramsey, Frank, Sr., 43
Ramsey, Sara, 43
Rancho Solano Private Schools (Peoria, Ariz.), 183
rebounding, 7, 41, 47, 55, 61, 73, 109, 143, 155, 195, 201, 207, 217
redshirting. *See* injuries
Reed, Ronald Lee, 65
Regis College (Denver), 69, 81, 85, 127
Reserve Officer Training Corp (ROTC), 44
Riley, Pat, 59, 71, 98, 142
Ritter, Goebel, 57
Rivals.com National Player of the Year, 217
Robert Morris University, 194
Robey, Fred, 112
Robey, Rick, 4, 7, 109–13, 120, 207

Robey, Sam, 109, 112
Rollins, Kenny, 9, 10
Rondo, Rajon, 175, 205
Roosevelt, Theodore, 76, 229n1 (chap. 10)
Rose, Gayle, 46
Rose, James Lawrence "Jim," 133
Rose, Judy, 133
Roselle, David P., 28, 30
Ruffian, 111
Rupp, Adolph, 11, 37, 126, 145, 167, 230n1 (chap. 11); 760th win and, 59; Ed Beck and, 49, 50–51, 52, 53–54; Larry Conley and, 69; Johnny Cox and, 58; death of, 60; "Fabulous Five" and, 3; Cliff Hagan and, 38; Joe B. Hall and, 76, 81, 84–85, 87–88; hiring of, 9; Dan Issel and, 75–77, 79; Wallace "Wah Wah" Jones and, 20, 21–22; William "Bill" Keightley and, 106, 163; mentors of, 4, 6; Charles "Cotton" Nash and, 2, 62, 63, 64; NCAA Championships and, 6, 48, 62, 86, 135; Charles Martin "C. M." Newton and, 27–28, 30; point-shaving scandal and, 10; Mike Pratt and, 93; Frank Ramsey and, 44, 45, 46; retirement and, 60, 76, 85, 86, 100; Rick Robey and, 110, 112; success of, as coach, 1, 6, 14
Rupp Arena, 7, 28, 38, 54, 108, 132, 133, 201, 221; jersey

retirement and, 17, 58, 148;
NBA preseason game and, 222;
opening of, 60; Wildcat fans
and, 134, 147, 167, 185
Rupp-Issel-Pratt Basketball Camp,
76
"Rupp's Runts," 59, 92
Russell, Bill, 33

Sacramento Kings, 195, 197, 207
San Francisco Warriors, 61
Seattle University, 11, 48, 55
SEC, 10, 63, 79, 198, 204; Coach
of the Year and, 81; Defensive
Player of the Year, 47; Joe B.
Hall and, 81
SEC Championships, 10, 25, 154,
231n3 (chap. 26); 1973, 60;
1993, 149, 150; 1994, 149, 150;
John Calipari and, 194; Joe B.
Hall and, 81; Ravi Moss and,
202; Adolph Rupp and, 85;
Orlando "Tubby" Smith and,
181
SEC Tournament, 155, 173, 198;
Academic All-SEC selection,
89; All-SEC honors, 89,
96, 124, 187, 196; Big East
Challenge, 221; John Calipari
and, 194; Co-Freshman of the
Year, 208; Defensive Player of
the Year, 196; Most Valuable
Player honors and, 149, 150;
SEC Player of the Year, 116,
194; Orlando "Tubby" Smith
and, 181, 182
Sendek, Herb, 157, 158

Sharman, Bill, 65
Shepherdsville High School, 81
Sheppard, Jeff, 161–67, 173
Sheppard, Stacey, 161, 164
Sims, Andy, 127
Sims, Glenn, 126–27
Sims, Marian, 126–27
Smith, Brian, 183
Smith, G. G., 181
Smith, Leon, 198, 203
Smith, Orlando "Tubby," 86, 181–
85, 189, 205, 231nn1–2 (chap.
26); Allen Edwards and, 169,
173; Chuck Hayes and, 195,
197; hiring of, 25, 30, 130;
Rick Pitino and, 181, 183, 184;
resignation and, 193
Smith, Ralph, 65
Smith, Saul, 181
Smith, Tanya, 189
South America, 160
Southeastern Conference (SEC).
See SEC
Southeastern Conference (SEC)
championships. See SEC
Championships
Southern Intercollegiate Athletic
Association championships, 9,
13, 14, 15–16
Sports Illustrated, 61, 92, 108,
230n1 (chap. 14)
Stamina (Anderson), 179
Stanfield, Kelly, 83, 84
Stanford High School, 16
Stanford University, 221
steals, 115, 175, 195, 217
St. Louis Hawks, 33

Stout, Louis, 127
Strickland, Rod, 220, 231n2
    (chap. 32)
Stuen, Leslie Ford, 151
Sullivan, Claude, 69
Sutton, Eddie, 129, 130, 140–41,
    142, 143, 146, 184
Sutton, Sean, 147
Syracuse University, 31, 130, 155,
    169, 175

Tate, Gene, 44
television, 7, 21, 57, 67, 92, 103,
    117; Wildcat fans and, 37–38,
    93, 100, 147
Temple University, 10
Tennessee High School, 123
Texas A&M, 193
Texas Tech University, 181
Texas Western University, 59, 67,
    68, 70–71, 92
Thomason, Bill, xii
Thompson, Bill, 37
Toronto Raptors, 195, 207
Towson University, 169
Transylvania College, 15, 25, 26
Tsioropoulos, Lou, 10, 46
Turner Broadcasting System
    (TBS), 103
Turpin, Melvin, 131

UCLA, 29, 86, 95, 211
UK Alumni Association, 50, 135
UK baseball, 19, 22, 25, 35, 41,
    46, 61, 64
UK basketball: 1948–1949 season,
    10, 81; 1949–1950 season, 10,
25; 1950–1951 season, 25, 27,
33, 41; 1952–1953 season, 10,
38; 1953–1954 season, 10–11,
33, 34; 1956–1957 season, 47,
50, 55, 56; 1957–1958 season,
47, 51; 1958–1959 season, 55,
56; 1960s and 1970s, 59–60;
1965–1966 season, 92; 1967–
1968 season, 89; 1969–1970
season, 74, 90; 1971–1972
season, 60; 1972–1973 season,
60, 96; 1973–1974 season,
96; 1974–1975 season, 95,
96; 1976–1977 season, 60;
1977–1978 season, 60; 1978–
1979 season, 115; 1979–1980
season, 115; 1981–1982 season,
123; 1982–1983 season, 123,
129; 1985–1986 season, 137,
138; 1986–1987 season, 129;
1988–1989 season, 25, 129–
30; 1991–1992 season, 130,
148; 1992–1993 season, 149,
150; 1993–1994 season, 149,
150, 155; 1995–1996 season,
130, 156; 1996–1997 season,
130, 155, 176; 1997–1998
season, 130, 162, 181, 231n2
(chap. 26); 2001–2002 season,
193, 195; 2002–2003 season,
169, 193, 195, 202, 204, 205;
2003–2004 season, 195, 196;
2004–2005 season, 195, 196,
202, 204; 2005–2006 season,
201, 205; 2006–2007 season,
193; 2007–2008 season, 207,
208; 2008–2009 season,

193, 207; 2009–2010 season, 194, 217, 220, 221; 2010–2011 season, 194; 2011–2012 season, 194, 213, 216; 2012–2013 season, 179, 187, 190, 194; athletic directors and, 25, 28–31, 35, 143, 183, 230n1 (chap. 16); earning degrees and, 10–11, 15, 28, 44, 46, 70, 75, 120, 166, 169, 172–73, 175, 185, 190, 211, 220; equipment manager and, 1, 106, 120, 163–64, 183–84; "Fabulous Five" and, 3, 9–10, 19, 36; "Fiddlin' Five" and, 11, 47; first college tournament and, 9, 13, 14, 15–16; games played and, 213, 214; games won and, 10, 23, 33, 34, 39, 45, 59, 193, 194; importance of in Kentucky, 1, 3, 54, 78, 91, 94, 113, 151, 157, 173, 209, 219; Kentuckians impacting, 2, 4–5; managers and, 126–27; "Rupp's Runts" and, 59, 92; staying for four years and, 53, 75, 107–8, 165–66, 211; three years' probation, 1989–1991, 25, 129–30, 143, 147; "The Unforgettables" and, 130, 143, 144, 148; "The Untouchables" and, 155. See also NCAA Championships; NCAA Tournament; SEC; SEC Championships; SEC Tournament; and individual basketball players and coaches

UK basketball recruitment, 3; Ed Beck and, 49–50; John Calipari and, 194, 217, 219; Johnny Cox and, 57–58; Allen Edwards and, 169, 171; Marquis Estill and, 189; Deron Feldhaus and, 147; Billy Gillispie and, 193; Jack "Goose" Givens and, 108; Kevin Grevey and, 101; Joe B. Hall and, 85, 86, 101, 140; Roger Harden and, 140; Chuck Hayes and, 195, 197; Derrick Hord and, 125; Charles "Cotton" Nash and, 63; Patrick Patterson and, 193; Rick Pitino and, 130, 161, 169, 171; Jared Prickett and, 157; recruiting and academic scandal and, 129–30; Rick Robey and, 113; Jeff Sheppard and, 161, 164; Orlando "Tubby" Smith and, 195; John Wall and, 217, 219
UK football, 19, 20, 21–22, 27, 30–31, 58, 220
UK Radio Network, 89, 92
"Unforgettables, The," 130, 143, 144, 148
U-19 World Championships, 213
University Heights High School, 201
University of Alabama, 25, 26, 27, 30
University of Alabama at Birmingham, 189
University of Arizona, 130
University of Arkansas, 129

University of Connecticut, 194, 221
University of Florida, 109, 112,
    159, 179, 194, 211
University of Georgia, 9, 13, 14,
    16, 181
University of Hartford, 217
University of Illinois, 132
University of Kansas, 4, 6, 60, 194,
    213
University of Kentucky. *See* UK
    basketball
University of Louisville, 7, 35, 36,
    81, 83, 86, 94, 129, 166, 184,
    189
University of Massachusetts, 151,
    193
University of Memphis, 193
University of Miami, 57
University of Michigan, 211
University of Minnesota, 181, 183,
    193, 197
University of Mississippi, 74, 79, 209
University of Missouri, 149, 151
University of North Carolina,
    Chapel Hill, 86, 190, 193, 201,
    211, 221
University of North Carolina,
    Charlotte, 89, 92–93
University of Notre Dame, 36, 86,
    90, 120, 125, 157
University of Pittsburgh, 135
University of South Carolina, 183
University of Tennessee, 21, 22,
    59, 73, 93, 117, 125, 133, 135,
    189, 231n1 (chap. 31)
University of the South, 81, 85,
    230n1 (chap. 11)

University of Tulsa, 181
University of Utah, 130, 161, 169,
    181
University of Wisconsin, 205
University of Wyoming, 169, 173
Unseld, Wes, 95
"Untouchables, The," 155
USA Basketball, 25, 27

Valdosta State University, 31
Valparaiso High School (Ind.),
    137, 140
Vanderbilt University, 25, 26, 28,
    59, 74, 183
Varnell, Lon, 84–85, 230n1 (chap.
    11)
Venezuela, 131, 133
Venture for Victory, 47
Vickers, Ryan, 164
Virginia Commonwealth
    University, 166, 169
Vogel, Frank, 159
volleyball, 169

Walker, Antoine, 159, 171, 203
Walker, Junior Kenny "Sky," 73,
    129, 132, 209
Wall, John, 137, 138, 217–22
Washington Bullets, 95, 101
Washington Wizards, 217, 221,
    222
Watson, Bobby, 45–46
Webb, Donald, 133, 230n1 (chap.
    18)
Webb, Dudley, 133
Webb, LaTanya, 169
Webster County High School, 151

Western Kentucky University, 35, 36, 57, 94, 169

West Virginia University, 194, 220

Westwood One Dial Global Sports, 102

Wethington, Charles T., 30

Wildcat fans, xi, 2, 6–7, 35, 63, 69; Derek Anderson and, 179; Ed Beck and, 54; Allen Edwards and, 171, 173; Marquis Estill and, 190; Deron Feldhaus and, 147; Travis Ford and, 153; Jack "Goose" Givens and, 107–8; Kevin Grevey and, 102; Cliff Hagan and, 37–39; Joe B. Hall and, 86, 87, 100; Roger Harden, and, 139, 141–42; Chuck Hayes and, 197, 198; Derrick Hord and, 125, 127–28; Dan Issel and, xii, 78–79; William "Bill" Keightley and, 1; Kentucky Colonels and, 80; Kyle Macy and, 120–21; Jim Master and, 134–35; Darius Miller and, 216; Ravi Moss and, 205–6; Charles "Cotton" Nash and, 64, 66; Charles Martin "C. M." Newton and,

30; Patrick Patterson and, 210–11; Mike Pratt and, 91–92, 93, 94; Jared Prickett and, 159; Rick Robey and, 112–13; Jeff Sheppard and, 164, 166, 167; Orlando "Tubby" Smith and, 184–85; John Wall and, 219, 221

Wildcat Lodge, 165, 221

Wildcats, Kentucky. See UK basketball

Williams, George, 177

Williamstown Junior/Senior High School (Ky.), 137, 142

Wilson, Mary Nancy, 37

women's basketball, 25, 103, 164

Woods, Sean, 143, 148

Word of God Christian Academy (N.C.), 217

World University Games, 213

World War I, 15

World War II, 36, 43

Xavier University, 84

Yahoo Sports National Player of the Year, 217

Yessin, Humsey, 27

About the Author

Doug Brunk is an award-winning journalist who holds journalism degrees from Point Loma Nazarene University and the S. I. Newhouse School of Public Communications at Syracuse University. He has written hundreds of articles for trade and consumer publications. A native of Rochester, New York, he spent his formative years in Wilmore, Kentucky, where he first played organized basketball and became hooked on following the University of Kentucky Wildcats men's basketball program. Brunk lives in San Diego with his wife and yellow Lab and is still trying to perfect his jump shot.